Building
An Altar Of
Sacrifice

FRANCIS ELIJAH NDUNAGUM

authorHOUSE®

AuthorHouse™ UK
1663 Liberty Drive
Bloomington, IN 47403 USA
www.authorhouse.co.uk
Phone: UK TFN: 0800 0148641 (Toll Free inside the UK)
       UK Local: 02036 956322 (+44 20 3695 6322 from outside the UK)

All scriptures in the book were taken from the KJV bible, unless otherwise stated.

Scripture taken from The Holy Bible, King James Version.

Published by AuthorHouse 07/14/2021

ISBN: 978-1-6655-9126-3 (sc)
ISBN: 978-1-6655-9125-6 (e)

Contents

Dedication

This book was borne out of a desire to empower God's people to fulfill their assignment here on earth knowing we were created by God and endowed with gifts to help humanity. This book stems from a deep desire to help Christians lead a fulfilled lifestyle and fulfill their walk and destiny. This book is a testament to the grace of God upon my life in my quest to provide biblical solutions and also serves to encourage, support and build up confidence in the lives of those who read it. I strongly believe that since this is an inspired writing, it will minister to some people who may identify with what I've put together.

It is with great respect and humility that I dedicate this book firstly to the Almighty God who is the source of my inspiration and to my wife 'Victoria 'Gift' Ndunagum who is true helpmeet in every sense of the word, always being there for me. To you my gift from God I say you have truly been a great woman and wonderful wife and life partner to me. You always encouraged me never to give up, but to dig deeper into my inner being to discover and develop the great gifts God deposited in me. You have truly been a great support, may God bless you richly.

To Pastor Dunni Odetoyinbo, Senior Pastor of Immanuel International Christian Ministries and also the founder and president of Women of Excellence International; a ministry set up to meet the needs of women of God worldwide, I dedicate this book to you. You have been a wonderful motivator, one who chose not to focus on people's weaknesses but rather identify with their potentials, encouraging them to harness the gifts in them and also thanking God for blessing humanity with their gifts. I have found you to be a true Barnabas unto every Paul of this generation. This scripture from Acts 9:26-27 could aptly be said of you "And when Saul was come to Jerusalem, he assayed to join himself to the disciples: but they were all afraid of him, and believed not that he was a disciple. But Barnabas took him, and brought him to the apostles, and declared unto them how he had seen the Lord in the way, and that he had spoken to him, and how he had preached boldly at Damascus in the name of Jesus," ({Acts 9:26-27})

I also dedicate this book to Bishop Erimujo who counsels me anytime I travel to Nigeria. I appreciate what God is using you to do in the life of young ministers.

I also dedicate this book to Apostle George my mentor and his wife Pastor Grace Akalonu. God bless you sir, you have been a good Daddy and mentor to me.

I used this opportunity to thank Rt. Rev Dr. Ngozi Durueke – Bishop, Power line Living Water Ministries for his support and loving heart. I dedicate this book to you.

I will not fail to mention Pastor Esther Davis Abdulai and Evangelist Theresa worthy instruments in God's kingdom that God has been using constantly to strengthen me and build up the brethren in the UK church (R.F.F.M), I dedicate this book to you.

Preface

The reason for writing this book is to help believers recognize the need to put God first in all their endeavours and to worship Him in spirit and truth. Having a spiritual understanding of what an altar really signifies is important to the life of a Christian.

In Gen 8:20, Noah set up the requirements for worship and offered up worship to God using some of the precious animals from the ark. This was the first thing Noah did before he attended to any other thing; Noah put God first.

Christians have in their worship a portrayal of Christ, not in an altar with sacrifices but in the emblems of the Lord's Supper {1Co 11:23-26}. This act which is symbolic, translates to Noah's act as priests of God {Rev 1:5-6}. Here Noah teaches us an important lesson.

Our whole lives as Christians are meant to portray Christ by consciously putting him first in everything we do. As Paul said, "I am crucified with Christ, nevertheless I live, yet not I, but Christ liveth in me; and the life which I now live in the flesh, I live by faith in the Son of God, who loved me and gave himself for me" {Gal 2:20}.

It is my responsibility as a believer to build an altar to the Lord in my heart, maintain and visit it daily. I take my sin, sorrow, faults, and failings to God at this altar and offer them as I would a burnt offering, allowing God's fire to consume them. I take my confidence, joy, and praise as peace offerings, willingly sharing them with my Master and continually submitting them to

Him. I call on the Lord at my altar, discussing my requests and desires with Him, and seeking His face for direction concerning them.

Finally, my altar is where God answers from Heaven by fire. Since my body is the temple and the altar is in the temple, I can never leave my altar unattended. As I maintain altar-consciousness and listen for God's voice, I will hear Him speak through His Word, through other Christian brothers and sisters, and even through observations of nature, which (after all) is the work of His hands.

I encourage you to cultivate an altar-consciousness by being mindful of whose you are by covenant. If you're just starting out, build your heart's altar to the Lord by making a determination to spend time with Him daily. To some, you may have to work at repairing your neglected and broken down altar. Don't be discouraged at the present state of your altar; take up from where you left off and do what needs to be done to repair it. If you've been regularly spending time with God, keep it up. Whatever the situation, it's a joy to know that God eagerly desires to spend time with us.

Jacob's Altar

(Jacob building an altar is a pointer to the fact that Christians can).

a. **Encounter**— (Jacob thought he was dreaming at first during his wrestling session at night until he 'woke up'. He had come into close contact with the creator of the universe in his night season. The altar he built from this experience was in part a monument to the first time he peered into the unseen realms in God.

b. **Access**— when Jacob woke from his dream, he realized it wasn't an ordinary dream, he had found the door to heaven; the place where angels were dispatched with heavenly communication to earth and from where they went back up bearing human petitions. If there was any place on earth where people could interact with God, to hear and be heard, this was the spot.

c. **Revelation**—"God is Awesome!" Jacob learned more about God than he knew before and also received clear direction on his life. The promises of the fathers would rest upon him, and God would be with him. Just as Jacob, God wants to reveal things to you but you must have a sound relationship with Him.

d. **Worship**— Jacob knew too well God was still at that place even when the dream was over. Since Jacob reckoned God was still at that place, he believed it was time to give something back to God as a token of his affection and love. He poured oil over his alter and worshipped God.

e. **Dwelling**— It wasn't just enough for Jacob that he had found God at that spot, he was determined never to let go of Him. He set up a stone as a memorial to demarcate the Bethel, the "house of God" that he had found.

We must have an altar which works for our own benefit. It is impossible to live for God with a carnal mind. The carnal mind is the enemy of God and is not willing to be subjected to the law of God. To be spiritually minded, one must continually stir up the gift of God that is within him.

If the Spirit which raised Christ from the dead dwells in you, it shall also quicken your mortal bodies." The Spirit must dwell and be maintained in us. This cannot be accomplished in its totality by simply attending church. One must maintain the fire upon his personal altar.

We must build an altar for the benefit of our children. A generation that does not know the Lord is a generation that cannot develop a relationship with the Lord. If we expect our children to worship, we must exemplify worship. If we expect our children to give offerings and pay tithes, we must do it ourselves. If we want our children to obey the commission and be witnesses, we must be involved in outreach. If we expect our children to pray, they must see us involved in prayer. Our homes should be an altar unto the Lord and a reflection of what we are commanded by the word of God to be and do.

We must build an altar for the benefit of the lost. There are some people whom we love who do not have a godly altar while some others who do, have neglected the care of theirs allowing it to fall into disrepair. They've probably done so by leaving the house of the Lord and going back to the lifestyle of sin from which they had been delivered We should be moved out of compassion to build an altar for those who have not built one for themselves.

Acknowledgments

1

What is Altar?

According to the Free Dictionary by Farlex, (he defines) altars as:

a. An elevated place or structure before which religious ceremonies may be enacted or upon which sacrifices may be offered.
b. A structure, typically a table, before which the divine offices are recited and upon which the Eucharist is celebrated in Christian churches.

According to Dictionaries - Baker's Evangelical Dictionary of Biblical Theology - Altar

A ltars were places where the divine and human worlds interacted. Altars were places of exchange, communication, and influence. God responded actively to altar activity. The contest between Elijah and the prophets of Baal involving an altar demonstrated interaction between Yahweh and Baal. Noah built an altar and offered a sacrifice to Yahweh. God smelled the aroma and found it pleasing. He responded to Noah's action by declaring that he would never again destroy all living things through a flood. In the patriarchal period, altars were markers of place, commemorating an encounter with God (Gen 12:7), or physical signs of habitation. Abraham built an altar where he pitched his tent between Bethel and Ai. Presumably at that altar he "called on the name of the Lord" (Gen 12:8). Interestingly, we are not told if there was a response. In the next passage however, Abraham went to Egypt and fell into sin, lying about Sarah out of fear of Pharaoh. There probably was no true communication at the altar between Bethel and Ai.

Webster's Online Dictionary Defines Altar as:

1. The table in Christian church where communion is given.
2. A raised structure on which gifts or sacrifices to a god are made.
3. A raised structure (as a square or oblong erection of stone or wood) on which sacrifices are offered or incense burned to a deity.
4. In the Christian church, a construction of stone, wood, or other material for the celebration of the Holy Eucharist; the communion table.

From this Scripture and based on my understanding, I will give my definition of an altar: "And Moses built an altar, and called the name of it Jehovah-nissi: For he said, because the Lord hath sworn that the Lord will have war with Amalek from generation to generation," Exodus 17:15-16, {KJV}.

My perception is this: an altar can be a place, an attitude or the moment in time when our thoughts and emotions are consciously directed toward God. "God is a Spirit: and they that worship him must worship him in spirit and in truth" {John 4:24}. An altar is a meeting point between the Higher being 'Almighty God, the creator' and the created lower being; humans. It is a place set aside and designated by human being as a place to worship to The Almighty God or gods. It is a place of prayer, a contact place with spirit(s) or the spiritual world; place of conversation, dialogue, and communication with spiritual powers. Here at this designated place, spiritual sacrifice(s) or covenants are made. God answers and blesses His people at the altar of every true prayer. The foundation for a successful Christian life and ministry is rooted in the altar of prayer. "And, behold, I send the promise of my Father upon you: but tarry ye in the city of Jerusalem, until ye be endued with power from on high," Luke. 24:49. An altar is a focal point for self-reflection and contemplation on the divine. It is a place where you make out time to dwell in God's presence as you worship or connect with God. It is where the person goes to pray, to be recharged, encouraged and be strengthened in faith.

Also, an altar is a divine place that enables Christians, families, and nations yield totally in submission to the Higher Power. It gives us the picture of what Jesus Christ the High Priest displayed on the cross by shedding His blood for the remission of our sin. It is at the altar you admit and submit your deficiency to the acknowledged supremacy of Jesus Christ the High Priest. An altar reveals the love and mercy of God and is a place where your heart can be broken as you hunger for Christ; worshipping Him in spirit and truth. It is here that self is crucified.

At this sacred place of the altar, you will receive deliverance from the attacks of the enemy. An altar is essential and non-negotiable to the true Christian. If we fail to build an altar or neglect to maintain the one we have, we will have no avenue of escape in times of crisis. Our progressive transformation into the image of Christ is fully accomplished at our altar as we let go and let God.

Issues such as unforgiveness are adequately dealt with on the altar. The reason we struggle so much with forgiving others is because it runs contrary to our human nature. When someone offends us, our natural reaction doesn't just stop at disliking the offence but we go further to crave and seek retaliation which is a natural attribute of sin. Forgiveness on the other hand, is contrary to the sin nature. It's much easier to bear a grudge than implement the law of grace and let go. God possesses great incommunicable attributes which we don't possess. Some attributes of God are solely peculiar to Him as He's described as: Omnipotent, omniscient, omnipresent, sovereign, and inspirational and we can never have any of these listed attributes.

However, there's a communicable side of God that we can have. God wants all of us to enter into a true sanctification process with Him so that He can begin the process of molding, shaping, and transforming us into the express image of His Son Jesus Christ. He wants to make us into a better and more holy people; transform us by the renewing of our minds, put right thinking into our thought process. God is love and we can allow this virtue to flow through us. He is merciful, longsuffering, and kind and He wants us to exhibit these qualities. God is forgiving and He certainly wants us to emulate that. His attribute of forgiveness was demonstrated through his death on the cross for our sins.

According to Dr Hasmukh Adhia, "To err is human but to forgive is divine".

Forgiveness involves consideration and tolerance. None of us would have come up to where we are today if our parents and others had not have forgiven our mistakes. No wonder, forgiveness is considered a virtue by most religions. There are umpteen reasons for forgiving.

One can be considerate if one is sensitive enough to understand why the other person is behaving in a particular way. For instance, if someone abuses you, you may react by slapping the person.

Rather if you chose to hold back, wait and watch instead of reacting immediately, you may soon discover that the person is a lunatic. If this were the case, would you still go ahead and retaliate, or choose to forgive?

Not forgiving means 'I retaliate'. Then the other person also retaliates. The fight then becomes endless and an unnecessary waste of energy. Is it not better to forgive once and close the account? Gandhi said, "Eye for an eye leaves the entire world blind." This does not in any way imply we allow others to exploit us and keep forgiving. One has the right of defense from repeated acts of cruelty, abuse or any provocative act. For example, if a friend or relative does such things always, one should be wise enough to distance oneself from such a person.

"Then David and the people that were with him lifted up their voice and wept, until they had no more power to weep. And David's two wives were taken captives, Ahinoam the Jezreelitess, and Abigail the wife of Nabal the Carmelite. And David was greatly distressed; for the people spake of stoning him, because the soul of all the people was grieved, every man for his sons and for his daughters; but David encouraged himself in the Lord his God," 1 Samuel 30:4-6.

An Altar could be a part of a building or a room. For instance the church serves as an Altar where Christians meet and fellowship with God. Men of

God in the Bible built Altars for God after He had done things for them; some examples are: Moses {in Exo. 17:15} Abraham, Isaac, Solomon e.t.c.

Altars, in the olden days were built with or out of stone where worshippers sought God's face and offered sacrifice of animals; but now our sacrifices are praise, thanksgiving and prayers through our Lord Jesus Christ unto God.

THERE ARE TWO TYPES OF ALTAR: {Spiritual altar 'N.T' and Physical altar 'O.T'}.

OLD TESTAMENT ALTARS:

These involve building physical altars. According to Old Testament records, an altar was built on a piece of land where you could kindle fire and burn the animal offered in sacrifice. While animals were a common sacrifice in the Old Testament; altars were used to sacrifice grain, fruit, wine and incense. God smelled the fragrance as the burnt sacrifice ascends unto Him and would come to grant the requests of those who had built the altar and offered sacrifices on it.

NEW TESTATMENTS ALTARS:

In the New Testament, we understand that an altar is a place of contact with God; as physical structures from where animal sacrifices were offered in Old Testament days we're no longer required. Jesus Christ is the ultimate sacrifice that puts us right with God and is ever making intercession for us. As a result, we do not require any further sacrifice of things to make atonement for our sins. "For the Law having a shadow of good things to come, and not the very image of the things, can never with those sacrifices which they offered year by year make the comers thereunto perfect...For by one offering he hath perfected for ever them that are sanctified," Heb. 10:1-14.

SCRIPTURE SPEAKS FREQUENTLY ABOUT ALTARS:

Altars were built for a number of different reasons.

An altar in the Old Testament was usually an upraised stone or earthen area with a flat top on which a sacrificial offering was made. Sometimes they were made of bronze, gold or wood. They were often used as a place of ministry to the Lord. However, not all altars were made for the purpose of ministering or sacrifice.

People build altars for different reasons. Some build them to honor their ancestors or remember a friend while some use them as creative kind of therapy. Others may build altars to support them in building a new life for themselves or to help them get through an illness or other challenges. Furthermore, some altars are built for support, others for release.

Some people use altars as centre points for mediation or ritual. Others build altars which are artistic or activist in nature. Some altars serve as memorials, while others are subversive. Some altars are built to honor deity, and some to honor self. Some altars are built at demonstrations, events and marches and can take on a very political tone.

It's good to study the various reasons why people built altars in ancient times and recognize the need for us to build altars in this present time. Man has a need to connect with God. In his quest to satisfy this inner need, the concept of an altar was created. The purpose of building an altar is to worship or connect with God and spirit guides. It is where the person goes to pray, perform rituals or simply recharge their internal batteries.

One of the things that we should note from the first altar builders is that they were people of great faith. It was very often as a result of their encounters with God that they built altars. And if we're to build an altar today, we must do this on the bases of our contact with Jesus Christ.

OLD TESTAMENT ALTAR BUILDERS:

a. Noah's Altar: Gen. 8:21-22; 9:1-3
b. Abraham's Altar: Gen. 12: 6-8; 13:17-18; 22:9
c. Isaac's Altar: Gen. 26:23-25
d. Jacob's Altar: Gen. 28:10-15, 16-19; 33:18-20; 35:1-7
e. Mosaic Altars: Ex. 17:15; 20:23-26; 24:4; 33:7-11

f.   David's Altar: 2 Sam. 24:18-25; Ps. 55:17

g.   Daniel's Altar: Dan. 6:10, 16, 22, 26-28

h.   Elijah's Altar: 1 Kings 17:1; 18:30-39, 42-45

i.   Balaam's Altar: Nu 23:1,14,29

j.   Joshua's Altar: De 27:4-7; Jos 8:30-32

k.   Reubenites and Gadites' Altar: Jos 22:10,34

l.   Gideon's Altar: Jud 6:26,27

m.   Samuel's Altar: 1Sa 7:17

n.   Saul's Altar: 1Sa 14:35

The first human altar builder – **Noah: Gen. 8:21-22; 9:1-**

AN ALTAR IS A SYMBOL OF GRATITUDE AND PROMISE:

Noah is the first recorded person to build an altar as is seen in *Genesis 8:20*.

Noah was expressing his gratitude to the Lord for providing a means of salvation from destruction, and God used the moment to make a promise to Noah that he would not again destroy all of his living creation.

The altar was a mark of joyous thanksgiving for the deliverance experienced by Noah and his family from the flood that had visited the earth. What made this altar acceptable to God was that sacrifices were offered to Him as an act of worship.

When Noah came out of the ark, he built an altar to God. When the aroma and incense of the burnt offering reached the mercy sit of God, He pronounced blessings and promised He would never again judge the world in the same manner - through a flood of water. Isaac and Jacob, son and grandson of Abraham, built altars wherever they went. Like Abraham, they knew in their hearts that they would only be safe when an altar was built. The altars were testament of their surrendered will and total dependence on God. It was the same with the kings of Israel and Judah. The good kings always raised and repaired broken down altars while the bad and ungodly kings tore them down.

Abram was an altar builder: **Gen. 126-8; 13:17-18**

A DISCIPLINE BELIEVER BUILDS A DIVINE ALTAR:

A careful study of the Old Testament will tell you that the patriarchs, starting with Abraham, built altars but not their own houses. They were contented to attend to God's altars and did not mind living only in tents. Abraham did not only build the most altars, but he also built the most powerful one when he offered his only son as the supreme sacrifice on Mount Moriah, {Genesis 22}. Little wonder he had such power with God.

Abraham's response, as recorded in the Bible, goes thus: *"So Abram went, as the LORD had told him"* {Genesis 12:4}. Looking back on this interaction thousands of years later, we marvel at Abraham's faith, at his trust, at his obedience. One wonders, given those same circumstances, would we have made the same choice? When you consider the culture in which Abraham grew up and his own upbringing, his decision is even more remarkable.

Abraham grew up in a society where multiple gods and idols were worshipped. In fact, Abraham's father, Terah, not only worshipped idols – he made idols. That was his business. And as the oldest son, according to tradition Abraham was expected to take over from his father and follow in the family business, becoming an idol-producer himself.

At a point in his life, Abraham came to realize that there was only one true God and that idols weren't the answer. He tried to help his father understand this as well. According to history when his father was out of the workshop, Abraham destroyed all the idols, except the largest one, next to which he put a stick.

When his father Terah returned, he was furious, and history has it that there was a contention between Terah and Abraham which goes thus: "What happened here Abraham, his father demanded. Abraham replied, "well, the big idol got angry at all the other idols and he destroyed them." To which his father answered, "That's impossible. He doesn't move. It's just stone." "Exactly, Father," Abraham said. "It is only a stone. There is but one true God."

Because of his faith and his willingness to stand not only against the cultural norms of his day, but also against his own father's believe. Abraham has been credited as the founder of only one God worshipper and he raised divine altars before God. He became the first person in the Bible to be called a Hebrew, and he became the father of a great nation – the Jewish people.

His bedrock faith in one true God is the very foundation upon which Jews and Christians alike have built our faith traditions.

No matter the challenges life throws at you as a child of God you should have a divine altar. Through this altar, you have the power to separate yourself from the iniquity of the world. No more excuses!

Everywhere Abraham pitched his tent, he always raised an altar. The altar is a symbol of self-sacrifice, self-denial and self-negation. His life spoke of the most intense devotion and deepest fellowship with Yahweh. His devotion to God was so intense that it appropriated all his personal ambitions and desires. He was totally sold out to God to the point that every time God demanded something from him, he offered a sacrifice on an altar he built. He had no reservations but responded with "Yes, Lord" when asked by God to offer his only son as a sacrificial object.

It costs when building an altar to God. Altars always are synonymous of death and sacrifice. Long after Abraham had left the place and moved his tent, the altar he raised to God remained as a testament to the spirit of his life: Total abandonment to God. Abraham actually spent one hundred years moving from tent to tent at God's command. He laid claims to nothing, not even to Isaac, the son born to him when he was 100 years old. He just held on to God in faith and obedience.

The first altar Abram built was an altar that resulted from an encounter with God as recorded in **Genesis 12:7; 13:4** and there he called on the name of the Lord.

In *Genesis 12:8* Abram builds another altar after moving to the mountains east of Bethel where he simply calls on the name of the Lord. Abraham built altars when he worshiped or when he moved from place to place. He raised an altar to the Lord or kept the existing ones he built functioning. Where ever he dwelt, the people of the land had their gods which they worshiped and built different altars for different purposes to them. But Abraham chose to build his altars to the Living God.

Abraham was the first man in the land to call upon the name of the Living God as "Jehovah". His action resulted in contentions with the demon gods that ruled over the land of the Canaan. Demons do not on their own rule a land; they can only do so in covenant with the people.

By building altars to the Living God, Abraham was consciously undoing the work of the enemy and also destroying the system the Canaanites used to worship their gods.

Altar also signifies possession as Abraham used building of altars in cities to claim the ownership of the lands for his children.

Altar connects to God and Angels. They serve as a tangible focal point and a gateway to peacefulness, where you can sit in solitude and peace and open your heart and mind to God. It is a point of contact for grounding and spiritual transformation.

The Patriarchs

Now we know why God called Abraham His friend. Friends must have common virtues and Abraham and God certainly had the same virtues. Both were loyal altar-builders, both loved their sons dearly and both dared to put aside their personal desires to offer their best on the altar for slaughter – Abraham, his son Isaac, and God, His son Jesus. Both knew the same horror and pain of having to give up their one and only son. Did Abraham turn his face away from Isaac as he set to thrust in the knife? God did - this is why Jesus cried, "Why have you forsaken me?"

One of the characteristics of a true friend is that they do not keep things from each other. They are intimate and open up to share the contents of their hearts. This was what God did with Abraham. Can He trust you enough to do the same with you? Three angels went to visit Abraham but only two left to execute judgment upon Sodom and Gomorrah while the third Angel, God Himself in disguise, stayed back to fellowship with the trusted altar-builder. God could talk with him because they both had much in common. He could share the burden in His heart with Abraham. Can God do the same with you? If you want that intimacy, build altars on which you will willfully sacrifice in obedience to His command.

The Kings

David and Hezekiah stood out also as prominent altar builders too. Judgment over Israel was turned away because David built God an altar on which he offered himself and his family as sacrificial objects to stay the plague in the nation. Judgment was turned away because God saw the selfless act: "And David spake unto the Lord when he saw the angel that smote the people, and said, Lo, I have sinned, and I have done wickedly; but these sheep, what have they done? Let thine hand, I pray thee, be against me, and against my father's house," (2 Samuel 24:17). The biggest revival took place in the days of King Hezekiah because he did not take the 'short-cut' route to revival. He carried out the difficult task of cleansing God's temple first. In a true revival, personal urge and selfish ambition must be dealt with first before proceeding to that of the society. When the personal sin of greed and self was dealt with, the people in Hezekiah's days were willing to 'shed blood' on the altar through an over-abundance of burnt-offerings and sacrifices to God borne out of their own free will.

2

Building an Altar

In the Old Testament there was no altar without sacrifices, significant in shedding of blood and death. Altars require blood for it is blood that sanctifies the altars; "And Moses took half of the blood, and put it in basins; and half of the blood he sprinkled on the altar," Exodus 24:6.

"And thou shalt take of the blood of the bullock, and put it upon the horns of the altar with thy finger, and pour all the blood bedside the bottom of the altar," Exodus 29:12.

"And he shall kill the bullock before the Lord; and the priests, Aaron's sons, shall bring the blood and sprinkle the blood round about upon the altar that is by the door of the tabernacle of the congregation," Leviticus1:5. This is the reason why a fleshly and carnal person sees it difficult to build divine altars. For them, it is impossible. Only people who are willing to deal with self or to pay the price can build divine altars in spirit and truth. In the book of Mark, Jesus said, "Whoever desires to come after Me, let him deny {die to self} himself and take up his cross and follow me" {Mark 8:34}.

There is no way we can raise a divine altar in our lives, if we do not die to self; to a selfish lifestyle and to self-government. In this present day materialistic generation of Christians, it will prove costly to build an altar unto the Lord because of the threat of 'self'. It is a pitiable generation – a generation that doesn't know how to raise an altar to God who have been ensnared in the trappings of life as a result of this void in their lives. Is it possible that God will ever bless a man or woman whose ways are not distinctly marked by the power emanating from their divine altar through prayers, intercession, worship and sacrifice? Will He ever grant favor to anyone who does not know how to honor Him as Abraham did? It is truly a challenge for a carnal, fleshly, calculative and self-controlled person to build a divine altar.

For us to build an altar, we first need to understand that:

You do not build an altar of covenant with God on the altar of Baal (iniquity).

You must start firstly by destroying the altar of wickedness in your heart as you come into true repentance. Jesus said, "....they that worship him (God) must worship Him in spirit and in truth," John 4:24. When this first step is taken, you can proceed to demolish the altar of Baal in your family, village or state, etc: With the destruction of each altar, you must build an altar to God in the exact same place where the ungodly altar had existed - 2 Chronicles 15:8.

Building an altar is a very important link in establishing powerful connection with God. Through this altar you are proving to God and to your subconscious mind that you want to connect and communicate with God. A godly altar is evident of your total surrender to God as His child.

Building an altar in a land spiritually stands for possession or ownership of that land. This is precisely what Abraham accomplished; possessing the land for his generations as he strategically built altars on it.

As a child of God, you can likewise posses the land for your generations by building altars on it. The bible: "Every place whereon the soles of your feet shall tread shall be yours: from the wilderness and Lebanon, from the river, the river Euphrates, even unto the uttermost sea shall your coast be," Deuteronomy 11:24 {KJV}.

It's necessary to know the origin of any project you are contemplating on embarking before you start out on it. This also applies to building altars. Though the name altar is not mentioned, the building of altars was first introduced by God in the Garden of Eden as a meeting point between man and God. It is in this place that man and God fellowshipped together.

Before I elaborate on the altar in the East Garden of Eden, I would like to state that the second place we can early identify an altar in the Bible is mentioned in Genesis chapter four {though the word altar is not used} where both Abel and Cane gave offering to the Lord. Abel's sacrifice was pleasing to the Lord but Cane's was not.

What's on Your Altar?

3And in the process of time, Cain presented some of his crops as a gift to the LORD. 4Abel also brought a gift – the best of the firstborn lambs from his flock. The LORD accepted Abel and his gift, 5but He did not accept Cain and his gift. This made Cain very angry, and he looked dejected. 6"Why are you so angry?" The LORD asked Cain. "Why do you look so dejected? 7You will be accepted if you do what is right. But if you refuse to do what is right, then watch out! Sin is crouching at the door, eager to control you. But you must subdue it and be its master." 8One day Cain suggested to his brother, "Let's go out into the fields." And while they were in the field, Cain attacked his brother, Abel, and killed him.

Some people do not see the need for an altar because they believe that the sacrificial death of Jesus Christ marked the end to sacrificial offerings. While animal sacrifices are not required of New Testament believers, there is a call for personal and spiritual sacrifices. With regards to offerings on our altars, we have two choices:

a. The offering of Abel which symbolizes humility and honor to God.
b. The offering of Cain which symbolizes pride and self accomplishment.

We all build altars and make sacrifices either to God or to self. These questions will help us know what we have on our altar.

i. Is your offering according to God's desire?
ii. Is your offering the best you can offer?
iii. Is your heart in the act of presenting the offering?

14

At the altar, God either receives or rejects our sacrifices. The heart of Cain is revealed in his offering. It is not pleasing to the Lord. God warns him to do well and be accepted. He warns him that sin lies at the door of his heart. Cain disregards God's words to him, grows angry and murders his brother. The first recorded murder stems from an altar of sacrifice. Altars have a way of revealing the content of the heart.

AN ALTAR IS A MEETING POINT WHERE GOD AND MAN OR ANGELS MEETS.

The place, at which God builds the altar in the Garden of Eden, is where He positioned the "Tree of Life". The Tree of Life stood in the centre of the Garden of Eden which elsewhere is called 'The Garden of the LORD or the Altar of God' Though it actually was a real tree, it was also symbolic of the fact that God was and is the source of eternal life and blessing for His people. Adam and Eve were to have their life centered in Him, even as the Tree was in the centre of His Garden.

There are other areas in the Bible that mention The Tree of Life. "And by the river upon the bank thereof, on this side and on that side, shall grow all trees for meat, whose leaf shall not fade, neither shall the fruit thereof be consumed; it shall bring forth new fruit according to his months, because their waters they issued out of the sanctuary; and the fruit thereof shall be for meat, and the leaf thereof for medicine," Ezekiel 47:12 {KJV}. In this verse, we read of trees whose 'fruit will be for food and their leaves for healing'. This image is reflected in Revelation, "In the midst of the street of it, and on either side of the river, was there the tree of life, which bare twelve manner of fruits, and the leaves of the tree were for the healing of the nations," Revelation 22:2 {KJV}. It is particularly clear in Proverbs where a number of things are referred to as 'a tree of life'; wisdom {Proverbs 3:15}, the fruit of the righteous {Proverbs 11:30}, desire fulfilled {Proverbs 13:12}, and a soothing tongue {Proverbs 15:4}}. The 'Tree of Life' in these scriptures symbolizes that which brings joy and healing to people.

"And the Lord God planted a garden eastward in Eden; and there he puts the man whom he had formed; Genesis 2:8 {KJV}. "Eden" literally

15

means pleasure, delight. The Garden of Eden was designed to be a perfect habitation for man; free of sin, it was a garden of pleasure and delight. Isaiah 51:3 describes it as the "Garden of the LORD", filled with joy, gladness, thanksgiving and the voice of melody. Because the Garden of Eden symbolizes all these, God took a decision to make it a sanctuary for man by putting man in it.

This explains why God quickly protected the "Tree of Life" when man sinned by sending Cherubims to guard it. Man was thus prevented from eating from "Tree of Life" in the altar. "So he drove out the man; and he placed at the east of the garden of Eden Cherubims, and a flaming sword which turned every way, to keep the way of the tree of life", Genesis 3:24, {KJV}.

TWO TREES IN THE GARDEN OF EDEN:

While the Bible teaches that there were many different fruit yielding trees in the garden, there were two trees that were of special significance, "And out of the ground made the Lord God to grow every tree that is pleasant to the sight, and good for food; the tree of life also in the midst of the garden, and the tree of knowledge of good and evil," Genesis 2:9 {KJV}. Although Adam was permitted to eat of the Tree of Life, which would have caused him to live forever {verse 16}, he chose not to eat of its fruit.

The Bible tells us that the 'Tree of Life' and the place called 'Paradise' still exist. "He that hath an ear, let him hear what the Spirit saith unto the churches; To him that overcometh will I give to eat the tree of life, which is in the midst of the paradise of God" Revelation 2:7 {KJV}. The Apostle John also saw the tree of life in the New Jerusalem descending to the earth after the Millennium, "...was there the tree of life, which bare twelve manner of fruits, and yielded her fruit every month: and the leaves of the tree were for the healing of the nations," {Rev. 22:2}. Redeemed man will once again be invited to eat of the Tree of Life.

Of the tree of the knowledge of good and evil, which some call the "temptation" tree, God specifically commanded Adam not to eat of it.

Why would God create a tree and then command Adam not to eat of it? This is a difficult question to answer. My understanding is this; for Adam to truly become a free moral agent, he had to be presented with a choice, either to rebel against God or obey Him. God requires that our love and obedience to Him be borne of out love, obedience and choice and not out of compulsion.

All men (including Adam) must understand that life is a gift from God. In other words, your life is not your own to do as you please. You were created for a Divine purpose and you have a destiny to fulfill. To prosper and live a successful life, you must train yourself to be obedient and trustworthy to the Lord by obeying His commands. The LORD clearly enumerated the consequences should Adam disobey Him, "…for in the day that thou eatest thereof thou shalt surely die." Until the moment of Adam's transgression, death did not exist in the garden. Once Adam disobeyed the Lord's command and tasted of the forbidden fruit, he experienced two deaths: a spiritual death, which was instant; and a physical death, which he experienced later.

Physical death is the result of spiritual death. Romans 5:12, "Wherefore, as by one man {Adam} sin entered into the world, and death by sin; and so death passed upon all men, for that all have sinned," The Bible makes it clear that the physical and spiritual consequence of Adam's sin was passed on to all mankind. Ecclesiastes 8:8 describes man's vulnerability to the power of death, "There is no man that hath power over the spirit to retain the spirit; neither hath he power in the day of death…" Death now reigned over all men until Jesus Christ was raised from the dead.

Another point of note is that Adam alone heard God's command not to eat of this tree; Eve had not yet been created. The Lord clearly expected Adam, as the head of the family, to communicate and enforce God's word in his family. Sadly, Adam failed miserably in this responsibility and his failure brought untold problems and hardship to the world.

Your duty as child of God should include passing down to the next generation the good, tried and trusted way of life you had received even as Paul rightly states "For I received from the Lord that which I also delivered to you: that the Lord Jesus on the same night in which He was betrayed took bread;" {1

Corinthians 11:23}. "They shall teach Jacob Thy judgments, and Israel Thy law; they shall put incense in Thy nostrils, and whole burnt-offering upon Thine altar {*Deut.* 33:10},

Adam's sin brought defilement to the altar. The spiritual altar became inactive while the physical altar was empty. Your spiritual altar could become inactive where the presence of God is absent due to your willful disobedience. If this occurs, you need to repair your altar firstly by repentance after which God's presence and glory will come back in.

When Adam sinned, he was driven away from the presence of God. The altar from where he fellowshipped with God was now defiled, consequently leading to his death. It wasn't God's plan for the soul he created to perish. God now had to perform a sacrificial atonement for redemption by using the blood of a slain animal. From this incidence, God taught Adam the process of atonement for himself through the blood of animal.

SACRIFICE:

A sacrifice is giving up something to God, most often represented in the killing of an animal.

In the Old Testament animal sacrifices were repeatedly made to cleanse or purify men from their sins of wrongful doings.

In the New Testament Jesus became that ultimate sacrifice, dying once and for all for the sins or wrongdoing of mankind. The sacrifice of Jesus is covered in all four gospels: Matthew 27:32-55, Mark 15, Luke 22:63-23:55, and John 19. Once Jesus died and was buried, he raised from the dead, proving his mastery over death and showing us that through him we can live a new life on earth. The maintenance of fellowship with Him will usher us into His presence in heaven. The book of Hebrews {chapters 7 through 10, especially Hebrews 10:1-18} connects the Old Testament sacrifices with the sacrifice of Jesus. We do know that no man made altar of wood or stone or precious metal can contain the presence of God.

Why did God specifically choose to sacrifice an animal in the East of the Garden of Eden and not another part of the garden for the atonement of Adam and Eve's sin? One reason is because "East of the Garden of Eden" is where the altar of fellowship between God and man is. Though an altar had previously been built, God killed an animal and used the blood to atone for Adam's sin and reactivate the defiled altar.

God wanted Adam to come to the altar of repentance and confess his sin, admitting his disobedience. Adam's disobedience to God translated to obedience to the devil. Before God killed the animal and used the skin to clothe them, Adam and Eve saw they were naked and covered themselves with leaves, implying they tried to hide their sin. The question is; can anyone truly hide their sin from God? No one can hide their sin from God. Though Adam and Eve covered themselves with leaves, God rejected their covering. He needed to let them know they were not able to make themselves acceptable to Him through the things they did.

We can't gain acceptance from God through appearances or works. God will not accept those who choose to follow their own path. Those accepted by Him are those who have made a decision to follow His only path. In accepting Him, He dwells in us by His Holy Spirit, leading and directing us daily in all our affairs.

Another reason God killed an animal to make clothes for Adam and Eve was to show them the death consequence arising from the disobedience of man.

The scriptures reveal to us that Adam and Eve did not put the clothes on themselves; rather God put the clothes on them. What God was showing them here was that only He could cover people, meaning our righteousness is imputed on us through the righteousness of Jesus Christ. Our self made righteousness cannot save us.

In the Old Testament, the people's sins were only atoned {i.e., covered} for. The book of Leviticus states, "For the life of the flesh is in the blood; and I have given it to you upon the altar to make an atonement for your souls; for it is the blood that maketh atonement for the soul," {Leviticus 17:11}. This Scripture speaks of the blood of animals which were sacrificed to temporarily cover the sins of the people of God in the Old Testament, until the coming of the Messiah who offered the perfect Sacrifice of Himself to God the Father.

In Hebrews it is written concerning Jesus, "Neither by the blood of goats and calves, but by His own blood He entered in once into the holy place, having obtained eternal redemption for us," Hebrews 9:12 (KJV). Jesus' blood did not atone for our sins; rather his blood did away with our sins forever.

JESUS' BLOOD SACRIFICE IS ALL SUFFICIENT

Hebrews 9:24-26 state, "For Christ is not entered into the holy places made with hands, which are the figures of the true; but into heaven itself, now to appear in the presence of God for us: Nor yet that he should offer himself often, as the high priest entereth into the holy place every year with blood of others; For then must he often have suffered since the foundation of the world: but now ONCE in the end of the world hath he appeared to put away sin by the sacrifice of himself." Jesus' blood applied to the Mercy Seat in Heaven is all-sufficient. Jesus only needed to offer Himself once as a sacrifice.

Jesus died on the cross, was buried to confirm His death, and then rose victoriously three days later. Christ is alive! Thank the Lord for His mercy, for paying for our sins with His precious blood.

The book of Colossians states, "In whom we have redemption through his blood, even the forgiveness of sins," Colossians 1:14, {KJV}.

It is Jesus' blood that cleanses away the sinners' sins. "And from Jesus Christ, who is the faithful witness, and the first begotten of the dead, and the prince of the kings of the earth. Unto him that loved us, and washed us from our sins in His own blood" {Revelation 1:5}. Jesus is a wonderful Savior! We owe him a debt of gratitude which cannot be adequately expressed with words. Christ has paid the price to redeem us unto Himself. Only a fool would deny the necessity of the blood for redemption. The death of Christ is important but would not have been sufficient by itself to redeem us. His blood had to be shed and applied to the mercy seat in Heaven.

Everything concerning our Lord Jesus Christ was leading up to the blood atonement in Heaven. Christ's death was absolutely necessary to validate the blood atonement; however, Jesus' birth would have been in vain if His blood had not applied in Heaven. The same is true of Jesus' sinless life, His death, His burial and His resurrection. These all would have meant nothing had Jesus not presented Himself before the Father in Heaven.

Jesus' sacrifice on the altar with His blood was the last sacrifice; we do not need to offer any other sacrifice unto God. Instead, we can build an altar of praise and worship on the foundational altar of Jesus Christ's sacrificial death.

3

Building a Family Altar

FOR WHAT REASON AND HOW MIGHT WE BUILD ALTARS TODAY?

We see that altars of old were set up as a memorial, for sacrifice, for interaction and personal revelation from God {God speaking}, a place where God would appear. They also served as a place for petition, thanksgiving and worship. The dealings of God amongst His people Israel serves as examples for us the present day church to learn from. All these things, scripture says, were written as examples for us "Now all these things happened unto them for ensamples: and they are written for our admonition, upon whom the ends of the world are come," {*1 Corinthians 10:11*}. The reasons for building altars cover the areas of both the personal and corporate expressions of our faith.

"Now therefore, fear the Lord, serve Him in sincerity and in truth, and put away the gods which your fathers served on the other side of the River and in Egypt. Serve the Lord! And if it seems evil to you to serve the Lord, choose for yourselves this day whom you will serve, whether the gods which your fathers served that were on the other side of the River, or the gods of the Amorites, in whose land you dwell. But as for me and my house, we will serve the Lord," {Joshua 24:14-15}

A family altar is a place from where the strategies and plans of God are enforced. It is a place where the evil designs of Satan and the kingdom of darkness are destroyed or altered by offensive and defensive intercession of families. It is the coming together of families to praise, worship and adore HIM for HIS faithfulness. It is a place where each family member receives strength. It provides a training ground for raising Godly families. Building a family altar ensures consistent family victory and marital bliss. The time dedicated to worship God in each home is a positive input that helps change the world.

Every Christian family should be a worship centre where the family come together to offer sacrifices to God. Many Christian homes suffer untold hardship today because members start and end the day without worshipping together at the family altar. Each family head must ensure that all the members of his family make it a point of duty to join in worship twice daily at the family altar. Its importance cannot be over emphasized. This is where Satan is kept away from the family.

It is possible to lose faith in God. Israel as a nation lost her faith in the God of her forefathers. So what can we do to try and prevent those following us from losing their faith?

THE FAMILY ALTAR

What is meant by a family altar? Family altar acts as a catalyst in helping to shift our thoughts from a busy life with all its attendant challenges and concerns to the spiritual realm. It serves as a healthy escape route from myriads of problems which may adversely affect our health. Family altars are points of contact between families and the living God. They are the interface which families can approach to render the contents of their heart thereby bringing about divine recognition by God and divine reconciliation with God. It is a regular place where a family can meet together within the home to pray to God, hear God speak to them through His word, receive revelation from God, worship and offer Him thanksgiving. As a regular practice it establishes a memorial to the activities of God in the lives of family members. Memorials result from God's activity on the part of His people in answer to prayers as well as the various ways God has provided and led the family corporately and individually. It gives a sense of collective identity as well as an understanding to the individual, of a God who cares; reveals and guides.

Children especially require such an altar. It should be established by every parent, whether single or married. When children can't read their bible, there are other activities that you can do with them to encourage worship, to build spirituality, and build memorials.

God has never underestimated the value of a family. After all, like marriage, He invented it. Family is the real society from which every other society comes out. This is seen in creation itself where it started in the book of Genesis. The redemptive history and the covenant of grace both indicate the vital role of family in God's calendar.

In a family, God shows the fundamental doctrine of His universal good government, but family life also reflects the principles of grace. The principle of representation is manifest in paternal spiritual headship, the principle of mediation in suffering and toil is seen in maternal child-birthing and child-rearing, and the mighty power of love is ideally manifest not only in the parental relations but in their wise and firm, but warm and gracious parenting.

The family is a special kind of household, ideally consisting of husband and wife, and children. It is the oldest and most basic of God's institutions for mankind. It is designed by God to be a spiritual entity and to provide for the training up of children into mature adult character.

A family has a built-in, divinely given authority structure. Parents are spiritual heads of families and leaders to their children. "And thou shalt love the LORD thy God with all thy soul, and with all thy might. And these words, which I command thee this day, shall be in thine heart: And thou shalt teach them diligently unto thy children, and shalt talk of them when thou sittest in thine house, and when thou walkest by the way, and when thou liest down, and when thou risest up," {Deuteronomy 6:5-7}.

Based on this great commandment, parents are called to impress on the hearts of their children a love for God. How can this be done? Through family worship, it is at this forum, parents talk about God and His word; who He is, what He desires from us who worship Him. The children should be made to know that God desires to bless every member of the family and not just the parents alone. In order to have a true picture of what Christianity actually involves, the meaning and expectation of the covenant relationship we have with God has to be taught to our children. They should understand that though promised, blessings are released to us in fulfillment of our obedience to His word, thus encouraging total obedience to God. To enable the head of the family, the man fully know how to steer the leadership of his family, it is necessary for him to ask God to give him a vision for the future of his family.

The Family is God's foundational block for society, it is therefore easy to comprehend why Satan and his evil government are determined in their effort to destroy the family and overthrow the institution of Marriage. God is not only the God of individuals but also the God of Families. He is a God of Generations as rightly described "And God said moreover unto Moses, Thus shalt thou say unto the children of Israel, The Lord God of your fathers, the God of Abraham, the God of Jacob, hath sent me unto you: this is my name for ever, and this is my memorial unto all generations," {Exodus 3: 15}. Moses wanted a revelation of God and God showed him that He is truly a God of Families.

God is determined to spread the knowledge of His glory from generation to generation within each family. The Psalmists said "Great is the LORD and most worthy of praise; his greatness no-one can fathom. One generation will commend your works to another, they will tell of your mighty acts" {Psalm 145:4}.

Satan's intention is to suffocate and destroy the knowledge of God in every generation; this explains the unrelenting attack on families on all fronts from the beginning of time. The Family in Christ needs to stand up and resist Satan in their homes, churches, communities and nation. Prayer provides the enabling factor in resisting Satan effectively, allowing us to take charge of our families, communities and nation for the Lord.

The place of Prayer. Prayer is a key that can release the life, power, mercy and grace of God over our families and at the same time, pull down strongholds of the enemy in our lives and circumstances, "For the weapons of our warfare are not carnal, but mighty through God to the pulling down of strongholds; Casting down imaginations, and every high thing that exalteth itself against the knowledge of God, and bringing into captivity every thought to the obedience of Christ," {2 Corinthians 10:4-5}. Prayer is the only solution to Satan's assault on family and society. Prayer alone releases the abilities of God to put right every wrong situation. How can we pray except we have a secret place, a high place, a divine altar?

We need to keep God at the center of our lives and activities. This is the very essence of a family altar. A family altar is an affirmation that God is at the center of the home, Christ being the head of this home. Christ is Resident and President and should be seen as such in the believing heart. At the family altar, every member of the family {saved and unsaved} is informed and reminded that God is at the center of their life. The home is meant to be God's place. It is a place set apart for God. You are reminding the family that the home is God's place and He is in charge of it. It is ordained to be a place of blessing through an obedient relationship.

Family altar is a listening and a learning ground. It is a place where the word of God is shared with family members; a place where family petitions are offered {concerning the home, school, work, health, etc.} You can present any situation before the Lord at the family altar because you have made Him the center of your being and affairs. This is God's place and it belongs to Him. We are looking to Him to protect the front door, the back door and the windows, all that is within and without.

This knowledge is important to the parent. If I pray and trust God according to what 1st Thessalonians 5:17 {"pray without ceasing"}, the family altar will serve as a reminder we need to be prayerful. As we give our family altar its rightful place, we will surely obtain the benefits. In the church, the Priest does teach and remind us how to "maintain family and private devotions; to educate our children in the Word of His grace and to seek the salvation of our kindred and acquaintances." Family altar is a time to get together to listen and to learn. It is a time to thank God, to petition to God, to praise God. It is a time to bring the problems to God and thanking Him in the knowledge that He is always available to us and is our very present help in time of trouble {Psalm 46:1}. We leave our problems before the Lord when we bring them to Him in prayer. If the problem involves the whole family, it is needful to pray together as a family. If family members are not in the place to do this, they will recognize that you are willing to deposit it with God. Family altar is a very specific place where this can be done. It is a place to remind everyone in the home that we have a great God in whom we put our trust, that God is more than able in every situation to give direction in any matter.

To have a good family altar, you have to work to ensure your heart is right. This involves getting to know God by His word, studying the word to have a deeper understanding, prayer daily to maintain your relationship with Him, doing everything He says to do. I pray we delight in God's Word all the time, "Oh, how I love thy law! It is my meditation all the day," {Psalm 119:97}.

To be a good example to our children, we have to live by the godly values what we teach them at our family altar meetings. "And thou shalt teach them diligently unto thy children, and shalt talk of them when thou sittest in thine house, and when thou walkest by the way, and when thou liest down, and when thou risest up" {Deut. 6:7}. Use each and every opportunity to teach the young ones about The Great God.

NEGLECTS

In this generation, family time around the Bible is increasingly being sidelined for hectic schedules. But we have a Scriptural mandate for conducting family devotions as recorded in Deuteronomy 6:5-7, "You shall love the Lord your God with all your heart, with all your soul, and with all your might. And these words, which I command you today shall be in your heart; you shalt teach them diligently to your children, and shall talk of them when you sit in your house, when you walk by the way, when you lie down, and when you rise up."

The New Testament admonishes in Ephesians 6:4, "And, you fathers, do not provoke your children to wrath, but bring them up in the training and admonition of the Lord."

God has placed the responsibility for the nurture of children in the hands of their parents. If parents do not provide the spiritual nurture, the world will raise them up in its ungodly standard. Children are facing tremendous pressures and influences in the world about them. The combination of school, friends, television, computers, and music floods and takes over their mind. Much of it has no regard for God and His plan for their lives. Through these avenues, they learn a great deal about the process of living, but not about the real purpose for living.

The purpose of the family altar is to inspire each family member with the truth that God is alive and is interested in our affairs. It is important to have family worship every day. The success of family devotions depends upon establishing a fixed time, and diligently adhering to it. Maintaining daily family devotions will not be easy. Satan will do his best to disrupt. Days will come when you will be tempted to say, "What's the use? No one seems to be benefiting." Success begins with a decision to do it, and then to follow through with it come what may.

Many families raise an altar of neglect when it comes to worshiping God together in the home. The writer of Hebrews raises a serious question: "How shall we escape if we neglect…?" {Hebrews 2:3}. Neglect what? Neglect to nurture our salvation. Neglect to nurture our children. Neglect is a most grievous sin.

If we neglect paying attention to material things from which we derive benefit, consider how devastating it would be to neglect raising a spiritual altar from where we connect with God the source of all life, for instruction, guidance, protection, sustenance etc.

A private devotion by any member of the family is commendable, but it will never produce the benefit and provide the corporate need of the family when they worship together. The family altar must first be established in the hearts of the parents, for they provide the leadership needed in this major project and adventure in the life of family members. It is considered a major project because the first most important church is the church in your house!

Family altar serves as a place of refuge and for sharing family problems. Children will hear their names mentioned with concerns by their parents, laid at the feet of the Heavenly Father; parents will hear their children pray for them in a way that no one else can. Thus the family altar is a highly needed aspect of every family. A number of values grow out of the practice of family worship.

1. **THE WORD OF GOD CAN BE EXALTED IN THE HOME THROUGH FAMILY WORSHIP:**

The Bible, the word of God, should consciously be exalted because it was given to us by the breath of God: "All Scripture is given by inspiration of God, and is profitable for doctrine, for reproof, for correction, for instruction in righteousness, that the man of God may be thoroughly furnished unto all good works" {2 Timothy 3:16-17}. The Bible should be exalted because it was written for our instruction: "For whatsoever things were written aforetime were written for our learning, that we through patience and comfort of the Scriptures might have hope" {Romans 15:4}. The Bible should be exalted because it is an unerring guide: "For the commandment is a lamp, and the law is a light, and reproofs of instruction are the way of life" {Proverbs 6:23}.

2. **A FAMILY CAN PRAY TOGETHER THROUGH THE MEANS OF FAMILY WORSHIP:**

In families where there is a daily praise of God in Psalms, hymns and spiritual songs and prayers, there is an additional influence on the young people. There are some men that have shown an example on how families can pray together through family worship. In the case of Joshua, he declared to Israel, "As for me and my house—we will serve the Lord" {24:15}. Neither the exalted office which he held, nor the pressing public duties which were upon him, were allowed to take off his attention from the spiritual well-being of his family. Again, when *David* brought back the ark of God to Jerusalem with joy and thanksgiving after discharging his public duties, he "returned home to bless his family" {2 Sam 6:20}. We think of the history of *Timothy* who was reared in a godly home. Paul called to remembrance the "sincere faith" which was in him, and added, "Which dwelt first in your *grandmother* Lois and your *mother* Eunice." Is there any wonder then that the apostle could say "from a child you have known the Holy Scriptures" {2 Timothy 3:15}!

"Pour out Your wrath on the heathen that do not acknowledge you—and on the families that do not call on Your name!" Jeremiah 10:25. We wonder how many of our readers have seriously pondered these awe-inspiring words! Observe what fearful threatening is pronounced against those who disregard worshipping God and obeying Him.

It is not enough that we pray as private individuals in our closets; we are required to honor God with our families as well. Each day, the whole household should gather together to bow before the Lord—to confess their sins, to give thanks for God's mercies, to seek His help and blessing. Nothing must be allowed to interfere with this duty. All domestic arrangements are to be put on hold during the specified worship time.

3. **DILIGENTLY PRACTICING THE FAMILY ALTAR WILL SET AN EXAMPLE FOR OTHERS.**

Paul wrote, "Ye are our epistle written in our hearts, known and read of all men" {2 Corinthians 3:2}. Or, as Jesus said, "Let your light so shine before men, that they may see your good works, and glorify your Father which is in heaven." We should let others know that we have a new life. Paul declares, "Therefore we are buried with him by baptism into death, which like as Christ was raised up from the dead by the glory of the Father, even so we also should walk in newness of life." The family worship time builds up our spirit man, our character and causes our light to illuminate this dark world. Engaging in the practice may act as an incentive for others to try the same good habit. A family can only practice this when they keep Christ as the centre of their home. "Except the Lord build the house, they labour in vain that build it." Psalms 127:1. "In all thy ways acknowledge him, and he shall direct thy paths." Proverbs 3:6. "And the peace of God, which passeth all understanding, shall keep your hearts and minds through Christ Jesus." Philippians 4:7.

This is the greatest rule. It really covers all others. Put Christ first! The real secret of true happiness in the home is not diplomacy, strategy, and untiring effort to overcome problems, but rather, union with Christ. Hearts filled with Christ's love can never be very far apart. With Christ in the home, marriage will be successful.

4. **FAMILY ALTAR HELPS TO KEEP THE FAMILY CIRCLE TIGHTLY CLOSED.**

"Thou shalt not commit adultery." Exodus 20:14. "The heart of her husband doth safely trust in her. ... She will do him good and not evil all the days of her life," {Proverbs 31:11-12}. "The Lord hath been witness between thee and the wife of thy youth, against whom thou hast dealt treacherously," {Malachi 2:14}. "Keep thee from the evil woman. ... Lust not after her beauty in thine heart; neither let her take thee with her eyelids. ... Can a man take fire in his bosom, and his clothes not be burned? ... So he that goeth in to his neighbour's wife; whosoever toucheth her shall not be innocent," {Proverbs 6:24-29}.

Family intimacies must never be shared with others, not even with parents. It is a great sin and a tragedy to break this God-given rule. Involving a third person to sympathize with or listen to complaints is a tool of the devil to estrange the hearts of husband and wife. Solve your home problems privately. Take every family problem to the family altar. No one else {except your minister or marriage counselor} should ever be involved. Always be truthful with each other, and never keep secrets from each other. Tell no jokes at the expense of your spouse's feelings. Vigorously defend each other, and strictly exclude all intruders. And as for adultery {in spite of what some marriage counselors say}, it always hurts the wronged spouse and everyone else involved. God who knows our mind, body, and emotional structure {and knows what helps or hurts us} says, "Thou shalt not." And when He says, "Don't," we had better not. Those who ignore His rule will pay the supreme penalty. So if flirtations have begun, break them off at once, or shadows may settle over your life that cannot be lifted.

5. CHILDREN CAN BE TAUGHT THEIR DUTY TO GOD THROUGH THE FAMILY ALTAR:

Many people wonder what the Bible has to say about teaching children. The Bible instructs God's people to teach children about God's laws. If people take the time to train their children about God's ways, children will not turn from that instruction later in life. Jesus valued children, and Paul provided additional support for teaching children about God in his writings in the New Testament.

Children should be taught to remember God in their youth: "Remember now thy Creator in the days of thy youth…" {Ecciesiastes 12:1}. Children should be taught to fear God: "My son, fear thou the Lord…" {Proverbs 24:21}. Children should be taught to obey God: "and {thou} shalt return unto the lord thy God, and shalt obey his voice according to all that I command thee this day, thou and thy children, with all thine heart" {Deuteronomy 30:2}. Teaching your children on how to obey God and his parent is the good and acceptable order of a family. This in turn impacts on the community and the wider society at large. No community or family can be prosperous where there is not due subordination in the household.

Teaching a child about God can result in a lifelong relationship between the child and God. In Proverbs 22:6, the Bible says, "Train a child in the way he should go, and when he is old he will not turn from it." Training a child involves multiple lessons in which a person teaches a child all about God.

The welfare of a child depends on the kind of teaching he receives from his parents; it is very important that a child should be taught early obedience to "law," as no one can be prosperous or happy who is not thus obedient..

One of the Igbo's traditions where I come from is, when a child is learning how to speak, it is the duty of parents to teach the child how to greet and respect parents, elders and welcome strangers. We do not reject strangers rather we receive and entertain them. When a child sees an elder on the road, what he does is to offer greetings to the elder, because he has been taught on how to greet elders.

In the book of Deuteronomy 6: 1-5, the reason why Moses taught the Israelites these commands was to enable them live reverent, respectful lives before God. They were also expected to hand down the teaching to their children and their grandchildren for them to do thus encouraging obedience. This would ensure they live long and happy lives. God calls believers today to walk in obedience too. As we model a life of righteousness, our children and their children will be influenced by our godly values, and God will bless us.

Children should be taught to honor their parents: "Honor thy father and thy mother that thy days may be long upon the land which the Lord thy God giveth thee" {Exodus 20:12'}. Paul states, "Children obey your parents in the Lord, for this is right. Honor thy father and mother, which is the first commandment with promise" {Ephesians 6:1-2}. Parents should not solely depend on the school for training their children. Children should be taught responsibility to parents while parents should understand that they stand in the place of God to their children, until they become old enough to know and serve God for themselves. Parents are required to see that their children yield the same obedience and submission to their will, as the parents yield to God. If this duty is performed by parents, they can then claim in faith and confidence the blessing of God upon their children. But if this duty is neglected by parents, God will hold them responsible, and the blood of their children will be required at their hands.

6. **THE FAMILY ALTAR IS A MEANS BY WHICH CHILDREN CAN BE WON TO CHRIST.**
Children should be instructed in the ways of the Lord: "Gather the people together, men, and women, and children, and the stranger that is within thy gates, that they may hear, and that they may learn, and fear the Lord your God, and observe to do all the words of this law" {Deuteronomy 31:12}. Children should be taught the way of salvation: "But as many as received him, to them gave he power to become the sons of God, even to them that believe on his name," {John 1:12}. "For by grace are ye saved through faith, and that not of yourselves, it is the gift of God" {Ephesians 2:8}. Through the family altar, children can be presented to Christ: "Suffer little children to come unto me and forbid them not, for of such is the kingdom of God. And

he took them up in his arms, put his hands upon them, and blessed them" {Mark 10:14-16}.

The children are hungry for God, the Living God who answers prayer and takes away their burdens of sin. Jesus commanded simply, "Go throughout the whole world and preach the gospel to all people" {Mk. 16:16}. The children are hungry for Jesus. He tells us to spread the Good News to everyone. We have fallen short of this charge by not obeying in feeding his lambs.

Children know how to pray and pray very well; Jesus even told us to follow their example and to become like them if we want to enter His Kingdom. What account will we give on the lives of the children entrusted to our care (since as parents, we are merely caretakers) when we appear before Him? Should we fail in our responsibilities; no excuse will vindicate us for not bringing them up according to God's word. From the scriptures, we understand we will suffer because of our faith in Christ. Let's read Peter's response when admonished to keep quiet at his appearance before government officials: "So they called them (Peter and John) back in and told them that under no condition were they to speak or to teach in the name of Jesus. But Peter and John answered them, 'You yourselves judge which is right in God's sight-to obey you or to obey God. For we cannot stop speaking of what we ourselves have seen and heard.' So the council warned them even more strongly, and then set them free" {Acts 4:18-20}.

Whereas, the word of God is both spirit and life to those who embrace it, "The Words I have spoken are spirit and they are life" {Jn. 6:63}, the words of the world work death and destruction to those who also embrace it. If we choose to feed our children with worldly language, we should not expect anything positive to come to them and out of them. We sowed the seed by the choice of our words. Knowing that all things were created through the spoken word and that what we sow is what we reap, parents need to sow only good and positive words and thoughts in the lives of their children and this begins at the family altar. Jesus loves the little children of the world. "And they brought unto him infants, that he would touch them: but when his disciples saw it, they rebuked them. But Jesus called them unto him, and said, suffer little children to come unto me, and forbid them not: for of such is the kingdom of God. Verily I say unto you, whosoever shall not receive the kingdom of God as a little child shall in no wise enter therein," {Luke 18:15–17}.

From these scriptures, we realize the opposition the children faced from adults in their attempts to get to see Jesus. Parents should ensure they do not create obstacles and stumbling blocks in path of their children's quest to know the Lord. According to the Scripture, the disciples were trying to hinder the children and Jesus rebuked the disciples and invited the children.

HERE ARE SOME HINDRANCES POSED BY PARENTS WHICH CAN STOP CHILDREN COMING TO JESUS:

THE PARENTAL UNBELIEF:

Some children are at a disadvantage if their parents are unbelievers. It is a herculean task for such children to come to God when their parents neither go to church nor believe in Jesus Christ. The bible declares "But the natural man receiveth not the things of the Spirit of God: for they are foolishness unto him: neither can he know them, because they are spiritually discerned," {1 Corinthians 2:14}. Unbelieving parents do not know nor understand scriptural principles which are the exact opposite of worldly standards and cannot therefore encourage their children to associate with groups whose beliefs are contrary to theirs.

Unbelief is a sin and this happens when people refuse to trust God. God is our maker, and he loves us. It is clearly wrong not to trust him. It is easy to believe things that are not true. We can see our problems but cannot see God. We believe we are in control of our own lives and can't see any logic in handing over control to someone we cannot see and whose capabilities we cannot assess.

When we think such thoughts, it is clearly sin and we are deceived by them. This confusion exists in our own hearts and minds. What we have in our mind is what we act out. Unbelief towards God and His kingdom is the picture presented here. This wrong attitude is what the Bible calls 'a hard heart'.

When the people of Nazareth heard Jesus preaches they were "astonished" by the wisdom he possessed. Yet, their unbelief blinded them to the plain truth of his identity; rather than see Jesus as their long awaited Messianic King and Savior, they simply saw Him as the village carpenter's son. Is there any part of Jesus' true identity you find it most difficult to embrace? There are passages of Scripture you need to read and know for the misconception to be done away with.

THE PARENTAL LACK OF KNOWLEDGE OF THE WORD OF GOD:

It is very sad when parents who once worshipped God turn their back on Him. Under such a home, there is no way the children can be raised with the fear of God when their parents have turned their back on God. When parents lack the knowledge of the word of God, it always turns into destruction in the family. It affects the spiritual lives of the children.

The warnings that God gave His people back then still apply to all of us in this day and age. The Bible says that God does not change, and this includes His ways and His word. The trouble is that most Christians are not conversant with these warnings because they have not spent time reading and studying the bible beginning from the Old Testament. Quite a few Christians can be classified as New Testament believers only having decidedly read the New Testament. Partial knowledge of the word of God is equally as dangerous to a believer as a complete absence of the knowledge of God is dangerous to the unbeliever.

LACK OF PROPER BIBLE TEACHING:

As a rule of life, we cannot give what we do not have. If a parent lacks sufficient knowledge of the word of God, this will be evident in their children's life. Lack of adequate parental bible teaching to children will either keep them out of the kingdom or weakens their usefulness in it.

It takes a far more proper understanding of a Biblical doctrine to be able to teach children than it does to teach adults. If you understand a thing very well, you can make it plain and transfer the knowledge to all levels of people including children. But if you are unclear in your own understanding, it will come across in your teaching of the subject. An inadequate knowledge of the word of God and His counsel is a great hindrance to the salvation and growth of our children.

HUMILITY AND YOUR ABILITY TO MINISTER TO CHILDREN:

In verse 15 of Luke 18 parents were bringing their infants to Jesus. The disciples rebuked them. Jesus counters this rebuke and encourages the parents to bring their children to him. He then warns the people by saying, "Whoever does not receive the kingdom of God like a child shall not enter it." In other words, when Jesus sees a person who does not receives His word with a pure heart as that of a child, he sees someone in danger of missing the kingdom because of pride.

If you receive the kingdom of God like a little child (with a child-like heart), you will not do anything to hinder little children from coming to Jesus. If you have a haughty spirit with a tendency of looking down on others, you will most probably be a hindrance to children. Kingdom attitude is to be child-like towards God. If do not have a child-like heart in God's kingdom, you are not teachable and are bound to disregard children in the kingdom.

There is an obvious connection between your humility and your ability to lead children to Jesus. The great hindrance to effective ministry to children is pride; and the great gift in ministry to children is humility.

Still, there are many other hindrances that we put in the way of the children as they come to Jesus. Most of these are in some way or other related to pride, though they don't look like it on the surface. Let's mention some of them and see how to do away with them.

THE LACK OF DISCIPLINED PLANNING

The effects of inconsistent child discipline or a total lack of any child discipline can create problems for the child. Children may feel insecure and develop anxiety and stress when there is a lack of consistent guidance. Children who do not learn appropriate boundaries when they are young experience difficulty with self-control later in life. This can lead to social problems and relationship issues as these children appear to be self-centered and expect to get their way at all times, never compromising with others. What may seem to be working at home in your child's early years can turn into a disaster against him when he's older and starts to experience issues of life.

Parents with the "I Don't Care" attitude, often transfer this attitude to their children. Overindulgent parents can create overindulgent children who feel that they are above the law and could not be bothered about the needs of others.

The best discipline will give your children a sense of what's right and what's not, without damaging their self-esteem and without being heavy handed.

Parents who fail to instill discipline in their children may not recognize how damaging it is for a child to lack boundaries to operate in. Without discipline, children will be deficient in the following important life skills evident in their conduct:

- Self control.
- Disrespect for their parents and authority figures.
- Bad and inappropriate behavior.
- Strong willed, selfish, and generally unpleasant to be with.
- Lack of social skills important for making friends example empathy, patience, and knowing how to share.
- Tendency to engage in negative behaviors that are harmful and even potentially dangerous for themselves as well as others.
- Being generally unhappy.

On the other hand, children who have been given firm but loving guidance have the following characters and abilities:

- They have more self control and are more self-sufficient.
- They are more responsible and enjoy "being good" and helping others at home, at school and in the world at large.
- They are more self-confident. They know their opinions and feelings will be heard, and that their parents love them even when they make mistakes.
- They know that they are accountable for their mistakes or misbehavior, and are more likely to make good choices because they want to, not because they fear punishment.
- They are pleasant to be around, and are more likely to have an easier time making friends.

Of course, *how* we discipline our children is equally as important as whether or not we discipline. Disciplining a child does not mean yelling or losing one's temper (though being human, all parents certainly have those moments when they get angry or frustrated by a child's bad behavior).

The key to positive child discipline is keeping your cool (and taking time out if need be) to be able to communicate with your child calmly about what is and is not acceptable behavior and how he can make better choices and learn from his mistakes.

Another hindrance to our children is the lack of disciplined planning especially in us parents.

What I have in mind is the fact that we often fail to teach our children not just because we lack understanding of what needs to be taught, but because we do not take the time to plan to teach. Periodically we feel guilty that our children are growing up so fast, but then we do not take the time to sit down and plan a strategy to take ten minutes a day to teach them the most important truths about life.

7. THE FAMILY ALTAR IS A MEANS BY WHICH CHRISTIANS CAN GROW IN GRACE:

"But grow in grace, and in the knowledge of our Lord and Saviour Jesus Christ" {2 Peter 3:18}. Anyone that calls himself a Christian should seek to be strong in grace: "Thou therefore, my son, be strong in the grace that is in Christ Jesus" {2 Timothy 2:1}. According to the Book of Joshua the Lord says, "This book of the law shall not depart out of thy mouth; but thou shalt meditate therein day and night, that thou mayest observe to do according to all that is written therein: for then thou shalt make thy way prosperous, and then thou shalt have good success," {Joshua 1:8}. Your daily reading of the Scriptures {God communicating with you}, and your daily prayer {you communicating with God}, helps to strengthen your inner spiritual lives and to guard you from being deceived by unprincipled men. This results in you being able to remain steadfast in the Lord as a result of you being solidly rooted in God's Word.

As we grow in the knowledge of our Lord Jesus Christ, we also grow in our love for Him. Increased knowledge of the Lord brings with it a greater understanding of what He did for us and cost. We develop an understanding of how great His love is for us, and realize His grace is a result of His love for us. Also, it helps a family to understand the finished work of Christ on the Cross which provides "the power of hope, liberty, freedom, recovery and restoration.

Grow in Grace and Knowledge

A Sermon on 2 Peter 3:18 by John M. Frame

This sermon is from the heart in a special way and I strongly believe after a lot of talking to God and searching his word, we should focus on it. This is the one passage of scripture that is presently crying out for priority attention. The subject is the one which is summarized in the last verse of our text: "But grow in grace and knowledge of our Lord and Savior Jesus Christ. To him be glory both now and forever! Amen" {2 Pet. 3:18}. Christian growth is the subject and our need.

Babies are cute and delightful in many ways. But if a person were to remain a baby for ten years or even more, it's an indicator that something is terribly wrong. A careful investigation into this awkward situation would reveal an abnormality in the baby and would consequently attract sympathy.

Now in the literal sense, there are no twenty-year-old babies. But there are twenty-year-olds, forty-, sixty-year-olds who often act like babies. And what do we say about them? That they are cute and delightful? Think of a grown man coming to church with a flower in his lapel that squirts water at you. You mutter, "Joe, why don't you grow up?" Soon Joe will find himself without friends because immature people irritate and are a real pain in the neck. Mature people cannot tolerate immaturity.

In the same way, it can be said that God is irritated at our immaturity. There are a lot of spiritual immature Christians in the church today. This is not necessarily a bad thing — much of it is due to God blessing our effort at evangelism, attracting new converts into our midst. The church has many young Christians who technically speaking should only remain immature for a season. But we've got to keep encouraging the young Christians to grow and not just be contented with the fact they've repented and given their lives to the Lord. Older Christians on the other hand never outgrow the need to grow in the knowledge of the Lord. We need to emphasize the basics of the gospel; salvation by the death and resurrection of Christ, salvation by God's grace {his free gift}, salvation by faith {not by anything we can do to earn it}. This basic knowledge of salvation is not just proper but essential too. In building any structure, the laying of a good and appropriate foundation determines the quality of materials used to build up the structure. A weak or faulty foundation will restrict the use of certain types of materials and with time, may result in the collapse of the building. You will observe here that the foundation is a part of the building and not the whole structure. Likewise, let's understand there is a lot more to learn in God's word beside the basics (foundation). The more revelation you have about the word of God, the more you're able to resist the devil and subsequently the more you occupy for the kingdom. It's sad when someone who has been a Christian for a long time knows nothing else than the simple gospel. This reflects in their language and attitude. They're not able to accomplish much for the kingdom because their understanding is limited.

Sometimes you find yourself in a situation where you just have to grow up fast. Someone attacks your faith, or gets to one of your children in college. You have to grow up fast. The book of 2nd Peter deals with this kind of emergency situation. Let's now look at it together.

These are the Apostle Peter's last written words to the church, and he knows that he is getting near the end of his life. In 2nd Peter 1:12-15 he talks about departing from his body, going to be with the Lord. Knowing about Peter's departure might not only have saddened the church but frightened it because of a revealed impending crisis. In chapter 2:1-3, Peter reveals about the invasion of the church by false teachers. This is bad news: "They will secretly introduce destructive heresies, even denying the sovereign Lord who bought them — bringing swift destruction upon themselves. Many will follow their shameful ways and will bring the way of truth into disrepute. In their greed these teachers will exploit you with stories they have made up."

How will the church survive this attack? How will the Christians be able to tell right from wrong in an age of theological confusion so much like our own? Well they can follow Peter! In 1st Peter 1:12 Peter declares he will keep reminding them of the truth, and in verses 16-18 of the same chapter he points out that his teaching is reliable: "We did not follow cleverly invented stories when we told you about the power and coming of our Lord Jesus Christ, but we were eyewitnesses of his majesty" {2 Pet. 1:16}. But someone says, "Wait a minute, Peter. You're not going to be here forever. You yourself have said that you're getting near the end of your life. Where do we go for guidance after you die?" Peter's answer: "Go to the Bible!" Verse 19: "And we have the word of the prophets {the Bible} — something more certain — and you will do well to pay attention to it, as to a light shining in a dark place, until the day dawns and the morning star rises in your hearts. Above all, you must understand that no prophecy of Scripture came about by the prophet's own interpretation. For prophecy never had its origin in the will of man, but men spoke from God as they were carried along by the Holy Spirit."

Now in chapter three, Peter gives them an example of the kind of debate they would have with false teachers. And he tells them how to use the Bible in that debate. He wants to stimulate the church to "wholesome thinking" {3:1} as they recall the teachings of the prophets and apostles, as seen in both the Old and New Testaments. Now, the false teachers will deny the second coming of Christ: "They will mockingly question; where is this 'coming' he promised? Ever since our fathers died, everything goes on as it has been since the beginning of creation" {2 Pet. 3:4}. That's an ancient heresy, but chapter 3 reflects a modern one. Lots of people today are saying exactly that. Oh, it sounds a little different. Today people say" There will never be a return of Christ or final judgment, because the world operates according to scientific laws or at least statistical regularities; and there is no scientific evidence that any cataclysmic judgment is in the works."

Can you refute that argument? Can you show what is wrong with it?

If you can't, you need to grow! Look what Peter says: "But they deliberately forget that long ago by God's word the heavens existed and the earth was formed out of water and by water." Did you know that? Did you know that the world was made, not only by God, but by God's Word? That's important. Did you know that the world was formed out of water, and that the Word of God kept the water and the dry land apart? Peter goes on to say in verse 6, "By these waters also the world of that time was deluged and destroyed"; Noah's flood. Verse 7: "By the same Word the present heavens and earth are reserved for fire, being kept for the Day of Judgment and destruction of ungodly men."

See what Peter is saying? He's saying that the most basic principle in the world is not scientific law, not statistical regularity, but the Word of God. The Word of God is what made the world in the first place. The Word is what brought the great past judgment of Noah's flood {the language almost suggests a de-creation}. And the Word will bring the next judgment by fire. The implication is this: it's to our own benefit to listen to God's Word about life, rather than taking heed to speculations made by scientists and philosophers.

Peter tells us that when we live by the Word of God, we learn a whole different way of thinking: "wholesome" thinking. Everything becomes different. This is a frequent theme in the Bible. Proverbs teaches us that the fear of the Lord is the beginning of wisdom, by deduction from this scripture; unbelievers have no wisdom at all. Paul in 1 Corinthians 1-2 says that the wisdom of God is sharply opposed to the wisdom of the world. Peter agrees. A Christian's understanding of biology is radically different from a non-Christian's understanding of the same field. A Christian's view on economics is radically different from that of a non-Christian view on the same subject. A Christian's perception of philosophy is radically different from a non-Christian's belief on philosophy. As Christians, we should not simply accept the fashionable thinking of the world because of its opposition to the word of God on many areas of life. We must think differently!

Not only must we think differently, but act differently. Peter says, "Look, if there really is going to be a second coming of Christ and a final judgment, how should we then live? Everything in this world will be burnt up. How should that affect our priorities?" Verse declares 14: "So then, dear friends, since you are looking forward to this, make every effort to be found spotless, blameless, and at peace with him." The Christian life is radically different from the non-Christian life. As Paul says {and Peter mentions that the false teachers twist Paul's letters}, "If any man be in Christ, he is a new creation! Old things are passed away, behold, all things are become new" {2 Cor. 5:17}.

Peter's conclusion: "Therefore, dear friends, since you already know this, be on your guard so that you may not be carried away by the error of lawless men and fall from your secure position" {2 Pet. 3:17}.

To prevent a falling away from the faith due to wrong and twisted interpretation of scriptures, and downright denial of what the bible tells us, we all need to focus on our growth factor and make it our priority as long as we're on planet earth.

So finally we get to our special text in verse 18: "Grow in the grace and knowledge of our Lord and Savior Jesus Christ." Grow in grace, grow in knowledge. I believe the first phrase includes the second. Growth in grace includes growth in knowledge. Let's look at growth in grace in general after which we'll get more specific and talk about growth in knowledge.

Grow in grace: All growth is by grace; it's God's gift. We must constantly ask him in prayer to enable us grow. We need God's grace, not only when we first believe in Christ, but we need it again and again; in our daily lives to make us the people God wants us to be. Are you as loving and kind as you wish you were? If not, you need to grow in grace. Are you hospitable? Do you open your home and share your belongings with others who are in need? If not, you need to grow in grace. Do you witness to the lost in some way? If not, you need to grow. Do you support the ministry of your church with your time and resources as you promised when you became a member? If not, you need to grow. Do you keep the Lord's Day holy, a special day for God and away from your own work and play? If not, you need to grow. Are you teaching your children, intensively, from the scriptures, giving them the knowledge they need to withstand false teaching? If not, you need to grow. Do you love to worship Jesus, so that you seek out opportunities to praise him? If not, you need to grow. Is the Lord Jesus the first priority in your life, so that to serve him you would count everything else as garbage? If not, you need to grow in grace.

Now the second aspect of this verse which Peter singles out here is a growth in the knowledge of our Lord Jesus Christ; knowledge that we need to combat the false teaching that swamps our culture today. How much knowledge do you have? Don't be satisfied with the simple gospel; there is so much more! If you rest content knowing only the simple gospel, you'll be powerless against the ingenious philosophies of the modern world. If you have inadequate knowledge about the word of God, Satan will definitely have a field day with your children because of their lack of knowledge on the word of God. There is so much to learn from the Bible. The more you study the word, the more you realize there is yet an even deeper level of knowledge to be tapped into.

There's the doctrine of creation in Genesis chapter 1. God made the whole heavens and earth out of nothing. Doesn't that blow your mind? And it's important in a lot of ways. You can't understand salvation very well without understanding creation. 2nd Corinthians 4:6 reads, "God, who said, 'Let light shine out of darkness,' made his light shine in our hearts to give us the light of the knowledge of the glory of God in the face of Jesus Christ." And Peter taught us that the de-creation of the world will be in many ways like its creation.

Then there's the doctrine of man as the image of God, in Genesis 1:26-28. Do you truly understand that? If not, probably you do not understand yourself the way God intends you to. On the doctrine of sin; do you know from what you have been saved? Do you know how black your sin is in God's sight? When you learn about this you'll be more thankful for your salvation. You'll praise God more loudly and you'll witness more fervently.

Concerning the doctrine of the covenant; would you say you know what a covenant is? These are the sort of things that sometimes fall through the cracks. We have to work at understanding it, making it an integral part of our thinking.

The covenant is the basic nature of our relationship with God. The covenant is the family of God. If you don't understand this it would hamper your understanding of the meaning of baptism and you won't understand where your children fit into the church.

There's the doctrine of the person of Christ. Have you ever wrestled with the question of how Jesus could be truly God and truly man? If not, you're not ready to present the gospel to World. And the work of Christ on the cross; how can one man's death bear the punishment for someone else's sins? A proper understanding of these attributes will help you explain this subject to your children or anyone who might ask you to shed more light on these aspects of Christianity.

We can go on in the same vain on these topics: regeneration, faith, repentance, justification, adoption, perseverance, glorification, the return of Christ and the judgment.

Can you work your way through all the many confusing teachings on these areas you listen to on TV, read in books, and hear from time to time on your own doorstep? You need to. You now see why it is pertinent for Christians to grow in the knowledge of God to avoid being ill-equipped thus acting as a hindrance to those coming into the kingdom.

God tells us we need to grow. He offers us his grace in Jesus Christ to change our lives and to enable our minds to understand and gives us the tools we need — his Word and the teaching ministry of the church — to impart to us what we need to know. I'll end, as Peter does, by ascribing to Jesus the glory both now and forever, Amen! He is the one whom we seek to know, and he is the one who supplies the grace we need to grow.

FAMILY ALTAR NEEDS COMMITMENT:

"Then the LORD said, 'shall I hide from Abraham what I am about to do? Abraham will surely become a great and powerful nation, and all nations on earth will be blessed through him. For I have chosen Him, so that he will direct his children and his household after him to keep the way of the LORD by doing what is right and just, so that the LORD will bring about for Abraham what He has promised him'" {Genesis 18:17-19}.

THE HEART→ THE HOME → THE ASSEMBLY {church} – these three areas are special to God and God manifests Himself in a special way in each of these areas. God can certainly be in the heart, "I am crucified with Christ; nevertheless I live; yet not I, but Christ liveth in me: and the life which I now live in the flesh I live by the faith of the Son of God, who loved me, and gave himself for me," {Gal. 2:20}. God can be in the home, "For I know him, that he will command his children and his household after him, and they shall keep the way of the LORD, to do justice and judgment: that the LORD may bring Abraham that which he hath spoken of him," {Gen. 18:19}. God certainly ought to be in His church, "The mystery of the seven stars which thou sawest in my right hand, and the seven golden candlesticks. The seven stars are the angels of the seven churches: and the seven candlesticks which thou sawest are the seven churches," {Rev.1:20}. "Unto the angel of the church of Ephesus write: These things saith he that holdeth the seven stars in his right hand, who walketh in the midest of the seven golden candlesticks," {Rev. 2:1}. Everything is in the presence of the omnipresent God, but enjoying His presence requires a healthy relationship with God by way of the cross.

The LORD has a defined purpose in establishing the family. The purpose is revealed to us by Prophet Malachi: "Has not the LORD made them one? In flesh and spirit they are His. Why one? Because He was seeking godly offering" {Malachi 2:15}:

One of Satan's greatest lies and weapon which some people accept is that it is impossible to build a godly family. The first family the LORD instituted, even in their fallen state did not fail God in raising a godly offspring— the righteous Abel. Although Cain, who was of the wicked one slew him, God raised in his stead Seth. Seth had a son and called his name Enosh who perceived that God was far from men due to proliferation of sin and wickedness. In his days men began to call upon the name of the LORD {Genesis 4:1-8; 5:25-26}.

The LORD saw ahead of Abraham into his descendants after him and spoke with the fullness of confidence that Abraham will lead them in the way of the LORD. We see the fulfillment of God's declaration concerning Abraham in all the scriptures.

Abraham is a believer, a worshiper of the living God. The LORD himself declared him righteous because he believed in Him, even in a seemingly impossible situation. What this reveals to us is that Abraham is a true worshiper of God and he built alters in acknowledgement of God's presence in every life occurrence. Isaac grew up and like his father; he became an altar builder too. He acknowledged the God of his father Abraham. Jacob also grew up to know the God of his fathers' Abraham and Isaac. He even called God "the fear of my father Isaac". He too like his ancestors became an altar builder, who knew the importance of worshiping the living God. We see a whole household declared for God. Even the servant of Abraham knew the God of his master and what He is able to do. He prayed to Him as he had seen Abraham his master do constantly {Genesis 24}.

In building our family altar we must make quality decisions as to what should take priority in our lives. The family comes second only after God who is undoubtedly our number one. The family comes before church, work or other social commitment. The family is primary and fundamental and should be covered with prayer and communion with God.

"I go the way of all the earth: be thou strong therefore, and show thyself a man; And keep the charge of the LORD thy God, to walk in his ways, to keep his statutes, and his commandments, and his judgments, and his testimonies, as it is written in the law of Moses, that thou mayest prosper in all that thou doest, and whithersoever thou turnest thyself: That the LORD may continue his word which he spake concerning me, saying, If thy children take heed to their way, to walk before me in truth with all their heart and with all their soul, there shall not fail thee {said he} a man on the throne of Israel" {1 Kings 2:2-4}.

David walked with God. Solomon was encouraged to walk with God. David reminded Solomon that if he and his sons {Rehoboam, etc.} would take heed and follow God, they would be blessed. Solomon had a great privilege that men in other homes did not have. He had a David in his home. Solomon was exposed to David. If Solomon made a conscious effort to represent God properly {verse 3}, his children would have an advantage in that they would follow after what they saw their father practice. Again we see the principles of 1st Corinthians 7:14, "For the unbelieving husband is sanctified by the wife, and the unbelieving wife is sanctified by the husband: else were your children unclean; but now are they holy". One believer exposes everybody to the possibility of the blessing of God! What they do with this privilege is up to them, but they have this privilege. They have the privilege of KNOWING GOD. They may use or abuse this privilege. The very best thing one can do is to develop the habit of being in God's presence and cultivating God's presence in them.

STEPS

    a.   Let the family be the most important focus of your life after God.

    b.   Reverence your partner and children and devote time to them {**1 Peter 3:1-7**}

c. Set time for your Family altar of fellowship with God once a week, daily or bi-weekly

d. Be willing to forgive and release your partner so that your prayers will not be hindered. {**1 Peter 3:1-7**}

e. Walk in the Spirit through Fasting, Meditation on the word and Praying in other tongues, building up your spirit man.

f. Determine to go all the way and make necessary sacrifices. If you fail re-set your will and continue in your walk with the Lord.

g. Do not forsake the gathering together of brethren {Family} {**Hebrews 10:25**}

h. Determine to give your children a godly heritage {**Malachi 2:15**}

ABRAHAM'S STRATEGY: RAISING PRAYER ALTARS BY 'WORLD TRUMPET MISSION'.

This is the strategy Abraham used to take the land of Canaan. Abraham went through the land and set up prayer altars taking the land for the Kingdom of the living God.

We should use this strategy to purge the land, prepare the spiritual ground and call upon God's presence. Success in the physical realm comes only after you have won the battle in the spiritual realm.

The people of the land had idols which they worshipped. They had different altars raised in different parts of the land, then came Abraham who used the same strategy of setting up altars to the Living God.

He was the first man in the land of idolaters to call upon the name of the Living God. He contended with the demons that ruled the land. It must be pointed out that demons do not rule the land unless they have a covenant with the people.

By building altars to the Living God, Abraham was undoing the work of the enemy. He was destroying the system the people of the land used to worship their gods. When he came back from Egypt after the famine, he continued with the ministry of re-establishing contact with His God by building new altars in the land.

This strategy did not stop with Abraham. This practice went on from generation to generation. Through this practice of raising altars unto God, they systematically purged the land and claimed it back for God. Raising altars signified contending with the gods ruling the land and displacing their reign with that of God. They were claiming back the land from the kingdom of darkness and handing it over to God. It took Abraham, Isaac and Jacob many years to purge the land and cleans the firmament above it.

Philip consistently built his family altar over time and succeeded in raising four godly daughters that could foretell the future.

If you want to have peace of mind concerning your children, you should raise a family altar. There is a need for you to arise and take your destiny seriously this year. It is only at the family altar that you can inculcate godly culture and values into your children.

God is calling us today and wants us to raise a personal altar in our heart. True prayer and worship starts in your heart. Your heart should be the first altar to call upon the name of the Lord. Other gods may have been unlawful tenants in our hearts. Some of these idols are: anger, bitterness, unforgiveness, jealousy, love of worldly things etc. These idols or negative attitudes crowd our hearts and affect our perception. Work must start in your life. As you yield your hearts, you can pass on the fire to others. We will call on God and surrender our hearts to Him, Romans 12:1.

THE SACRIFICES NEEDED IN THE FAMILY ALTAR ARE:

☐   Songs of praises

☐   Stories of God's provision

☐   Recounting times of personal encounter with God.

☐   Teaching how to pray.

☐   Read Bible stories; stories with Biblical principles or children's devotionals

☐ As the children's knowledge increases, have them read a passage of scripture and share its meaning collectively.

☐ Keep a book of petitions and answered prayers.

☐ Having family altar time with the children. Different times work for different families.

☐ Spiritual development of the family is important and the church just cannot do it on one hour per week in Kid's church. The main responsibility goes to the parents.

☐ **Deuteronomy 6:4-9:** Let's individually and corporately build altars in our lives…things which remain for the generations to come!

4

Building Personal Altar

" I BESEECH you therefore, brethren, by the mercies of God, that ye present your bodies a living sacrifice, holy acceptable unto God, which is your reasonable service," {Romans 12:1}.

Your personal relationship with God begins at the moment you have your personal altar time, realizing your need for Him, admitting you are sinner and by faith receiving Jesus Christ as Saviour.

God our heavenly Father has always desired to be close to us, to have a relationship with us. Before Adam sinned in the Garden of Eden, both he and Eve knew God on an intimate personal level. They walked with Him in the garden and talked directly to Him. Due to sin, we were separated and disconnected from God, "But your iniquities have separated between you and your God, and your sins have hid his face from you, that he will not hear," {Isaiah 59:2}.

At this point, I would like to stress the need for the personal altar in relating with God. How do we as individuals hear from God today? How does God reveal Himself to me as an individual? Is worship my lifestyle? Is my sacrifice actually shaping my character? Do I call on God for the needs of others, not just my own needs, and how do I build memorials in my life? If not, is the church worldwide losing its ability to build faith for ourselves and the generations to come? Throughout the ages, mankind has misunderstood the manner in which God should be approached. You need to have a practical, personal, present relationship with God. You need to have a personal relationship with God that is daily maintained and daily exercised. How is your own personal prayer life? How is your own personal devotional life? What kind of quality time do you spend with God? Do you spend time on your knees before Him? A humble position by a humble heart for heavenly business with the Most High God is always unique. One's heart, attitude and action toward his personal altar are the key.

If you allow yourself to be disconnected from your personal altar of divine intimacy with God, you put your life in danger. The plan of the Devil is to lure you to sin and weaken your spiritual life and render you ineffective. If you allow the devil to succeed in doing this to you, it means he would have succeeded in bringing you under his control.

You need to cultivate the habit of spending time in devotion with God, not just at your convenience. Most of us do not know how to have a devotional relationship with God because of these two reasons; we don't recognize the importance, we don't know how to. We are all tied up with ours personal needs--etc.

It is amazing how just one verse meditated upon can refresh us, help us to re-focus on the Lord and set our course straight. This is what we need; every internalized truth results in making wise decisions. This self development carries us through our crises moment because we are well informed by the word of God. Apart from seeing us through crises moment, our knowledge of the word prevents us from falling into traps as we daily pursue the will of God in all we do. Little wonder the Bible says, "And be not conformed to this world: but be ye transformed by the renewing of your mind, that ye may prove what is that good, and acceptable, and perfect, will of God," {Romans 12:2}.

Our personal altar of worship is a navigator that helps us to ask these questions:

1. Who am I?
2. Where did I come from?

3. How is my relationship with the Lord?
4. What will the Lord say about me?
5. What is the purpose of my life?

Have you allowed God's Word govern and guide you? Are you able to take God's Word and correctly apply it when crisis comes? Many fail to do this. The key to doing this is to learn to live by the word in your day to day life. In moments of crisis, you will be ready to put your faith in God's word to work. Living by the word of God gives you a better quality of life and grants you victory in trials. Though many claim they live by the word of God, they interpret the word wrongly and are not able to live victoriously nor do they live a good quality of life as Christians.

In the Scripture we have two men who approached God with an offering, and yet only one received God's approval. The men were performing an act of worship but with entirely different motives as we shall soon discover by taking a closer look at the passage. Cain presented an offering that was self satisfying while his brother Abel presented an offering that was pleasing and acceptable to God. Don't ever let the offerings on your personal altar be a 'self satisfying' offering.

It should be noted, that while New Testament believers are not required to present animal sacrifices on an Altar, they are required to approach God in worship which is 'sacrifice'. In both Testaments, the faithful followers of God set their hearts and minds on seeking both the will and the favor of God. Hebrews 13:15 speaks of an Altar of God whereon we offer the sacrifice of praise to God continually, that is the fruit of our lips giving thanks to His Name. Hebrews 13:16 continues with our offerings by stating, but to do good and to communicate {or share} do not forget; for with such sacrifices God is well pleased. The Altar is the place where God and man meet together; the place where our wrongs are atoned for. Christ's sacrifice for all humanity was final and this sacrifice was pleasing and acceptable to God. If we approach the Altar of God with any other sacrifice other than that of the Perfect Lamb of God, Jesus, neither we nor our offering will not be accepted. We need to understand that Jesus Christ is the propitiation {or the atoning sacrifice} for our sin according to 1 John 2:2, 4:10. Without

Jesus Christ, there would not be an opportunity to come to the Altar of God or please Him in any way. God's Altar was made accessible through the death of Jesus Christ. This significance is what the offerings of Cain and Abel represented. Abel understood that if He was to bring an offering, the offering had to satisfy God and not himself. Cain, for whatever reason, paid no attention to God's requirement and rather chose to approach the Altar of the Holy God with a desire to satisfy himself. Both men came to the right place, but one man left dejected and angry. Both men offered a gift, but one man's gift failed the test of pleasing the LORD. Not everyone that gives an offering in the Church pleases God in doing so and such an offering stands rejected by God.

The ultimate sacrifice a man can present to God through his personal altar is a yielded and broken heart that responds totally to the will of God. It is on this platform of a right heart that an altar can be initiated, completed and a quality sacrifice brought to the living God. If the sacrifice is big, precious and expensive and the heart is not yielded, changed or broken, it is not accepted of the Lord. Do you want to offer a quality sacrifice to God? It has to come from your heart. Why not give your heart to God now?

Personal Altar: As the name implies, this is a personal means of communication and fellowship with God. It is otherwise known and called 'Quiet Time'. This is a time you have assigned, committed, set aside for God to meet with you on 'one-on-one' basis. It comes with a specific time at which you seek the face of God through worship, praises, thanksgiving and prayer. The essence is to hear and talk to God; it ensures a direct link with God, "And he withdrew himself into the wilderness, and prayed" {Luke 5:16}. Family or Home Altar is a place where family members meet for the purpose of communing, fellowshipping, praising, worshipping and praying to God. It comes with a specific time of meeting.

People who build and offer what God desires on their altars never get discouraged by, nor become victims of the forces of darkness. An altar is a place {not necessarily physical} set apart for interaction with the spiritual. It is a place where the lives of men are empowered as seen in Psalm 91.

One's progress in life depends on the power of his altar. If you don't raise a personal altar, you'll become a victim of another man's altar.

Understand that the 'altar' principle is not exclusive to Christianity. In a typical traditional African setting, each child has an altar built for him by his parents. It is on this altar that prayers, incantations, and most importantly, sacrifices are made for him until he gets to a reasonable age, when he's left with the responsibility of running his altar. Quite evidently, those families that take their altars seriously lead more notable lives and stand out in the community.

The altar concept is also seen in other religions. This lends credence to the fact that one's personal altar is the root of his spiritual life. The deeper your root, the taller your life grows; the more resilient you become, the more you flourish, and consequently the more relevant you are to your world –just like the palm tree. The bible in Psalm 92:12 clearly tells us "the righteous shall flourish like the palm tree". The palm tree has extremely deep roots which not only supports its height but enables it to stand firm trough all types of weather.

Essentially, it is the sacrifice that makes an altar. Without sacrifices, an altar is powerless. Access to the spiritual realm always has a cost attached to it. This is why spiritual men like David said "I cannot appear before God empty-handed."

What sacrifices are you laying on your altar? Your altar is the place you first dedicate your offerings, tithes, and your seeds to God before bringing them to church. How seriously do you take your altar?

The story in Genesis 12:8 and 13:3-4 inform us this altar was built between Bethel and Ai. The implication here is that worshipping God and calling on His name in His House, an appointed place of worship keeps your life from ruin.

If we don't have an altar of worship at home from where we worship God personally and with our family, we will not be able to worship as part of a congregation. These people tend to blame the church leadership for failing to put their lives right for them, but fail to realize the fault comes from them for failing to build a personal altar of personal worship. Some people find it difficult to worship God when they're passing through difficult times because their altar of worship is weak.

Job is one of the men I admire and respect in the Bible. When I look at Job's worship, I'm convinced he must have built a strongly personal altar of worship with the Lord. He learnt of the devastation which befell him concerning his sons and daughters who were feasting in their oldest brother's house. A great wind struck the house, destroying it and utterly killing all of Job's ten children "While he was yet speaking, there came also another, and said, Thy sons and thy daughters were eating and drinking wine in their eldest brother's house: And, behold, there came a great wind from the wilderness, and smote the four corners of the house, and it fell upon the young men, and they are dead; and I only am escaped alone to tell thee,"{1:18-19}. The messenger said he alone escaped to bring the report to Job. He may have been one of the servants of Job's son and it is possible Satan allowed these four messengers to remain alive to take the devastating news which were all brought in quick succession to Job. Satan designed these incidences to totally devastate Job that he in turn would curse God and reject Him.

Satan's plan failed because Job instead arose and tore his robe {a sign of repentance}, shaved his head, a picture of his being exposed before God in a condition of weakness, then fell to the ground in humble prostration before his Creator. Job's response in the face of calamity implies a denial of self. Last and most important of all is the fact that he chose to worship, giving God the place of highest honour and dignity {vs.20}. To those who have no faith in the living God, worship is one thing they would never consider. The natural reaction from those who have no faith in the living God would be to complain bitterly that they do not deserve what has happened to them. Many today allow themselves to be deceived by selfish motives that energize Satan, rather than being moved by a true response of faith to all the bitter experiences of life. Job's words should deeply impress themselves on every Christian "Naked I came from my mother's womb, and naked shall I return there. The Lord gave, and the Lord has taketh away. Blessed be the name of the Lord" {vs.21}. A person with complaining attitude will never change issues for the better, while a person with thankful heart will be greatly blessed in the end.

Job's attitude serves as an example to show Christians how to handle difficulties rather than use their challenge as an excuse for sinning! "Looking into Job's case, he did not sin nor accuse God foolishly" {vs.22}. Many since Job's time have endured terrible afflictions and trouble. Rather than alienating them from God, their troubles have driven them into His presence to find comfort and joyful communion with the Lord. Job still had much to learn and his response to trouble shows the reality of his faith and worship in the Lord.

HAVING DEVOTION ON YOUR PERSONAL ALTAR:

We should find a regular place for personal altar devotion.

"And in the morning, rising up a great while before day, he went out, and departed into solitary place, and there prayed," {Mark 1:35}. Jesus' early Morning Prayer devotion shows us the depth of his humility. Rising up so early in the morning to pray meant that His first thoughts were on His Father. This also shows his intense desire to commune with his Father.

The greatest transactions of a man's life are made, not in a church, but behind closed doors.

In order to grow in grace, we must be cultivate an alone time with God. It is not in society that the soul grows most strongly, it is in your private corner where you are in contact with the Lord. Every believer needs to know the Lord's specific plans for his or her life. One quiet hour of prayer will surely guarantee much more progress than time spent in clubs, parties, and village meetings. It is in the desert that the dew falls freshest and the air is purest.

A personal praying devotion on your altar will make God very personal in one's life. Here, one learns to relate to God, hear from God directly, and not through others who may likely take undue advantage of your inability to hear from God for yourself. Great servants of God were noted for engaging in private devotions.

Here are some examples of men of old who developed a strong relationship with God. Isaac meditated in the field at evening, "And Isaac went out to meditate in the field at the eventide; and he lifted up his eyes, and saw, and, behold, the camels were coming," {Gen 24:63}.

David prayed three times daily, meditated on his bed at night - Ps 55:17; 63:6

Daniel's custom was to pray three times daily - Dan 6:1

Having personal altar devotion helped these servants to grow in the knowledge and understanding of God and His ways. Likewise, through your altar you learn more and more about how to defend the faith; stand up for Jesus as soldiers of the cross! In addition, you will be fortified against the assaults and attacks of the wicked one, and fortified against deception.

The most important kind of knowledge you gain from your personal altar devotion is not information, but a relationship. What I mean is recognizing the difference between knowing someone and knowing about someone. Here at your altar you personally get to know the risen Christ. You get to know He did not only die to be your Saviour, He arose to be your friend and companion. Your knowledge about Him can be both truthful and relational.

Your growth in knowledge will not be complete until you know the love of Christ which passes knowledge as recorded in Ephesians 3:19 "And to know the love of Christ, which passeth knowledge, that ye might be filled with all the fullness of God". "And the peace of God, which passeth all understanding, shall keep your hearts and minds through Christ Jesus," {Philippians 4:7}. "O the depth of the riches both of the wisdom and knowledge of God! How unsearchable are his judgments, and his ways past finding out!" {Romans 11:33}.

Only then will you be filled with greater joy and hope in your Christian walk in your sojourning here on earth. If you spend a little time daily with the Lord in your altar and in studying of His Word, you will desire more and more to be with your Lord. As you spend more time with the Lord, you also desire more and more to see His return on the clouds of glory.

REASONS FOR HAVING PRIVATE DEVOTIONS ON YOUR PERSONAL ALTAR

The answer is simple and comforting. God has graciously chosen to give us the privilege of being His partners in both the physical and spiritual areas of life. Through prayer, we work with Him in defeating the powers of evil and in bringing about the fulfillment of His loving purposes in the world.

A. **TO DRAW NEAR TO GOD...**
   1. God is found by those who seek Him
      a. David's advise to his son Solomon - **1Ch 28:9**
      b. As Azariah told king Asa - **2Ch 15:2**
   2. God draws near to those who draw near to Him - **Jm 4:8**

-- Do you want a closer walk with God?

B. **TO RECEIVE SPIRITUAL NOURISHMENT...**
   1. We need spiritual nourishment in our lives - **Mt 4:4**
      a. Man cannot thrive on physical food alone
      b. We need spiritual food that nourishes the soul
   2. Spiritual growth comes from the Word of God - **1Pe 1:23; 2:2**
      a. We are born again through the incorruptible seed
      b. We continue to grow by the Word of God
   3. God's Word provides spiritual strength - **Ep 6:10-17;** cf. **Psa 119:7-11**
      a. We need God's help to fight our spiritual battles
      b. The Word of God provides such help!

-- Do you want a stronger, spiritual life?

C. **TO FIND PEACE AND STABILITY...**
   1. We live in a world filled with anxiety; prayer provides the antidote - **Php 4:6-7**
   2. We live in a world filled with pitfalls; God's Word keeps us from falling - **Ps 119:105,165**

-- Do you want inner peace and outer stability?

GOD CHOOSES OUR ALTARS

Psalms 37:23 says, "The steps of a good man are ordered by the LORD: and he delighteth in his way." May we be encouraged every time we come to our personal altars. Living for God sincerely and truthfully is a strong pointer to the fact that our steps are ordered by the Lord. Submitting and offering ourselves to the Lord prospers us spiritually. But if we neglect attending to our personal altars, we will not only fail to grow spiritually, but we will be placing ourselves in spiritual danger.

How do we recognize the fact that we are facing an altar? When you come in contact with a situation you are powerless to change; powerless here meaning *if* you are determined to stay within God's will. An example could be a situation where someone has lied about you. Or it could be a situation where you are required to do something which is against your belief, difficult or unpleasant. It could be a situation where you are not getting what you had set your heart upon. There are many ways of escaping the 'unpleasantnesses of an altar experience, but you would have to step out of the will of God to do it.

This is what makes it an altar, because whatever the situation may be, an altar by its nature is always uncomfortable. It always has a certain amount of emotional pain to it and has never been something we enjoy having to go through.

Mary the mother of Jesus was told through prophecy that a sword would pierce through her own soul {Luke 2:35}. This was fulfilled when she stood helplessly watching as her son was despised and rejected of men, arrested and brutally beaten, nailed to a tree and left to struggle in pain. Can you imagine what was going on inside of her? Was she tempted to get angry at God? Was she trying to devise a way to rescue Him from His passion? I doubt it. That experience was a divinely-ordered altar for her which she had been told to expect. I believe she resolutely submitted to it.

This is what an altar experience does for us. It pierces our soul, cuts deeply into our inner man; It strikes at the thoughts and intents of the heart and is designed by God to slaughter everything that is of the flesh. This is why it hurts. It can be agonizing and unbearable. Time slows down when you're on the altar. We just want to spend quality time in His presence and we dare not try to end it too soon. Not until the Lord says, "It is finished."

Keeping track of how you spend your time with your personal altar can be of great value in evaluating the relationship of your time with God. Record the number of hours spent on business, class, sleep, Christian service, recreation, etc. Place the total hours per week used in each activity below.

Giving your time to God as a Christian is important. You cannot expect God to move in your life if you do not spend time with him. Spending time with the Lord means appreciating who He is to you. As a Christian, your daily priorities should include spending quality time with God. When you wake up, before undertaking any household chores, you should go before God and sanctify the day. Ask him to order your steps. Worship him and just enjoy loving on him. You will realize that when you wake up and start the day with God, the whole day falls in order. "There is therefore now no condemnation to those who are in Christ Jesus, who do not walk according to the flesh, but according to the Spirit: For as many as are led by the Spirit of God, these are sons of God," {Romans 8:1,14}.

The only way God is going to reveal to you His will for your life is only if you spend time with Him. This should not be a quick prayer in the morning as you get out of bed followed by another two words of prayer during lunch time when blessing the food. You have an intimate relationship with God and as part of this relationship; you need to spend quality time with Him. Give Him your time and you will be amazed at how much you will accomplish in the day.

God wants to reveal to you His treasure house. He also wants you to know how much you mean to Him. When you give your time to God in prayer and reading the Word, you will be amazed at how easily you are able to conquer giants that have been keeping you down. If you fail at this relationship, you won't make any remarkable progress in your Christian life. You can only have a personal encounter with God at your own altar, not on another person's altar.

5

Principles for building Altar

To build an altar you have to apply certain principles, the requirement in building an altar. You must credit God for whom He is and give Him His due. Enthrone the Lord as head of your home. Let his local assembly be your priority, even as it is His. Help your family know the limitless possibilities in God, His conduct, competency, the comfort found in Him etc. In a nutshell, let your family know the nature, the character, and the attributes of God as you meet at your family altar. Worshipping God should not be limited to good times but should include bad times too. It's at a time like this that we really need to hear from God, receive a word of comfort, hope, direction, instruction to keep help us navigate through the trying time.

God desires to make your heart His home. His word should dwell richly in your heart that He may show up in any situation you call on Him. The bible makes us know that God and His word are one and the same.

GENUINE SALVATION

"Who shall ascend into the hill of the Lord? Or who shall stand in his holy place? He that hath clean hands, and a pure heart; who hath not lifted up his soul unto vanity, nor sworn deceitfully," {Psalm 24:3-4}

To build an altar, you need to be genuinely saved through Jesus Christ as salvation cannot be found in any other than in the name of Jesus Christ. "Neither is there salvation in any other: for there is none other name under heaven given among men, whereby we must be saved" Acts 4:12.

Salvation is a free gift of grace received by confession of faith. It requires total submission and surrender of every area of life to the Lordship of Christ coupled with a willingness to worship Him in spirit and truth.

Genuine Salvation takes only place when a person completely surrenders to Christ's Lordship at the moment of confessing Him as savior. Partial surrender is not a genuine salvation.

The scripture reveals the necessity of having a full understanding of acknowledging Christ as the Lord and Master of one's life in the act of receiving Him as Savior.

"For by grace are ye saved through faith; and that not of yourselves: It is the gift of God: Not of works, lest any man should boast. For we are his workmanship, created in Christ Jesus unto good works, which God hath before ordained that we should walk in them. Wherefore remember, that ye being in time past Gentiles in the flesh, who are called Uncircumcision by that which is called the Circumcision in the flesh made by hands; That at time ye were without Christ, being aliens from the commonwealth of Israel, and strangers from the covenants of promise, having no hope, and without God in the world. But now in Christ Jesus ye who sometimes were far off are made nigh by the blood of Christ," {**Ephesians 2:8-13**}.

In Scripture we see an example of a genuine salvation that took place in someone who was searching. In Acts 8:26-39 we read about a Eunuch who as a result of concerns he had over his spiritual life, travelled great lengths to worship. But no matter what he did, he felt unsatisfied. He had known his salvation would not come through riches, position, or religion because he had it all. Despite his standing and affluence in his society, he was still spiritually dissatisfied.

Unfortunately this Ethiopian represents many today who are religious, read the scriptures, seek the truth, but are still spiritually dissatisfied. They are sincere in their religion and in their quest for God, but are lost still!

Just like the Ethiopian, they go to church week after week to try and fill the void in their life but repeatedly leave church empty. The missing link is that these ones have not connected with God through Jesus Christ, hence the perpetual void in their lives. It's only the Lord Himself who can fill this void. Why not invite Him into your life to empower you have a richly satisfying life, a life with meaning and purpose. The Bible says to "Seek ye the LORD while he may be found, call ye upon him while he is near: Let the wicked forsake his way, and the unrighteous man his thoughts: and let him return unto the LORD, and he will have mercy upon him; and to our God, for he will abundantly pardon. For my thoughts are not your thoughts, neither are your ways my ways, saith the LORD. For as the heavens are higher than the earth, so are my ways higher than your ways, and my thoughts than your thoughts" {Isaiah 55:6-9}.

You have to put your faith in Jesus as you ask Him to forgive your sins and save your soul. Merely turning a new leaf without confessing your sins and inviting Jesus into your life as Savior and Lord is not enough and does not indicate you have a relationship with the Lord. Your sins must be dealt with! You need forgiveness from the only one who can forgive sins, Jesus Christ. Turn to Jesus Christ in faith, trusting upon Him alone as your only way to Heaven, "Jesus saith unto him, I am the way, the truth, and the life; no man cometh unto the Father, but by me," {John 14:6}. Have you, yourself done this? Remember, only Jesus paid for your sins on the cross, so only Jesus can forgive those sins and save your soul from Hell.

When we are convinced and convicted of sin, godly sorrow enters the heart. The Apostle Paul declares that "godly sorrow worketh repentance unto salvation" {II Cor. 7:10}, and also states that there can be no pardon without such repentance.

PASSION FOR GOD:

"And behold, I propose to build a house for the name of the LORD my God, as the LORD spoke to my father David, saying, Your son, whom I will set on your throne in your place, he shall build the house for My name," {1 Kings 5:5}. Solomon did what is fore-fathers could not do.

As Christians, our passion in life should be living God's way. We have been given the awesome opportunity to be members of God's own family. What else could be more exciting, inspiring and worth devoting our lives to? Having a passion for this gift we have been given shows our appreciation and devotion to our Giver. Learning of God's way of life and His awesome plan for mankind should motivate us and propel us to action instead of being mere hearers of His word. "But be doers of the word, and not hearers only, deceiving yourselves. For if anyone is a hearer of the word and not a doer, he is like a man observing his natural face in a mirror," {James 1:22-23}.

It's good and necessary to have the knowledge about God, His kingdom, His ways and what is expected of us as kingdom citizens but the attitude of our hearts which He alone sees, determines the outcome of our relationship with Him. Living God's way just because we have to isn't pleasing to God; He wants us to live joyfully. God, unlike man, looks at the heart, "But the LORD said to Samuel, "Do not look at his appearance or at his physical stature, because I have refused him. For the Lord does not see as man sees; for man looks at the outward appearance, but the LORD looks at the heart,"" {1 Samuel 16:7}. He wants us to obey Him because we want to—because we love Him. Colossians 3:23 says, "Whatever you do, do it heartily, as to the Lord." Our obedience to God and His commands should be something we do with our whole heart, something we do with passion.

PASSION AND WILLINGNESS IS THE ULTIMATE ATTITUDE TO SERVING GOD.

Willingness is a motivator to passion. Passion without willingness is like a car without fuel, the car can't move. It is also like a preacher who doesn't have the Holy Spirit in him. The passion and willingness you have for God drives you forward to live the life He has for you. Also, having the passion and willingness for God strengthens your confidence and self-esteem. Passion and willingness encourages one to persevere over obstacles.

King Nebuchadnezzar decided he was worthy of worship and made a proclamation to the people. They were to pay homage to his golden image whenever he wanted them to. "That at what time ye hear the sound of the cornet, flute, harp, sackbut, psaltery, dulcimer, and all kinds of music, ye fall down and worship the golden image that Nebuchadnezzar the king has set up. And whoso falleth not down and worshipeth shall the same hour be cast into the midst of a burning fiery furnace," {Dan 3:5-6}.

Shadrach, Meshach and Abednego didn't respond; they didn't get angry, nor did they say anything against the King. Rather they said, "If it be so, our God whom we serve is able to deliver us from the burning fiery furnace; and he will deliver us out of thine hand, O king. But if not, be it known unto thee, O king, that we will not serve thy gods, nor worship the golden image which thou hast set up," {3:17-18}. Rather than engage in self pity because of the life threatening decree promulgated by Nebuchadnezzar, in which he forbade the worship of any other god except the idol, these Hebrew children continued to pray to God, not minding the death sentence. The penalty for anyone caught going against the king's order was death by fire - the worst kind of death. They were caught and delivered to the king who was really angry with them for challenging his authority. "Then Nebuchadnezzar full of fury, and the form of his visage was changed against Shadrach, Meshach and Abed-nego: therefore he spake, and commanded that they should heat the furnace one seven times more than it was won't to be heated," {verse 19}. From this scripture, it is evident that our passion to serve God determines how far our faith overcomes any temptation facing us.

Satan hates it when believers are faithful and turns up the heat to deter them. Nebuchadnezzar gave orders to make the fire seven-times hotter and had his most valiant men throw them in the fire {verses 20-22}. The furnace was so hot, his men perished, but not the victims of his wrath; people who continued to praise God in the face of imminent death. These three Hebrews boys had an unparallel passion for God; they believed, trusted God, and would not compromise their faith.

We should be watchful not to be like the church at Pergamum that resisted persecution, but they began to fall to seduction. With overwhelming cultural pressure around them, they began to compromise. They look for pleasure in physical things of the world, and it cost them greatly in spiritual things. Jesus told them to repent.

These young men knew the testimony of how God delivered their fathers from the land of Egypt and brought them into the Promised Land, Canaan. They remembered what God did in the land of Egypt, how; He brought them through the Red Sea and this greatly motivated their faith to believe and worship the one and only true God.

In the New Testament period according to the book of 1 Corinthians 2:1-5, Paul was putting the truth across to believers concerning the message he preached. The cross was not only his primary subject; it was also his motivation for living. When we begin to understand all that Jesus did for us at Calvary, we have the passion and motivation that will enable us live for Him.

A person without passion and willingness has no more value than a candle without a flame or fire without light. Passion with willingness is a burning desire that creates commitment to a person's life. Look for a great successful person and you will see a person full of passion and willingness. Doors that are locked for a man without passion and willingness opens for those that have passion and willingness.

THE MAN THAT HAS A HEART FOR GOD IS THE MAN THAT HAS A VISION FOR THE WORLD.

The man that has a heart for God is the man that has a vision for the world. Paul had a heart for God and today we can see his vision for the world. "Then Paul stood up, and beckoning with his hand said, Men of Israel, and ye that fear God, give audience. The God of this people of Israel chose our fathers, and exalted the people when they dwelt as strangers in the land of Egypt, and with an high arm brought he them out of it...And afterward they desired a king: and God gave unto them Saul the son of Cis, a man of the tribe of Benjamin, by the space of forty years. And when he had removed him, he raised up unto them David to be their king; to whom also he gave testimony, and said, I have found David the son of Jesse, a man after mine own heart, which shall fulfill all my will," {Acts 13:16-22}.

The passion and willingness of Paul in serving God helped him to leave a testimony behind. Have you ever pondered at what your loved ones will write on your gravestone? What words would you want inscribed there?

In this Acts 13, the apostle Paul tells us God's evaluation of David: He described him as "a man after His own heart, who will do all His will" {vs. 22}. This is an awesome testimony of a life well lived! The Lord wasn't describing a perfect man, but one whose life was centered on God's interests and desires.

The messages of David according to the book of Psalms attest to the fact that his relationship with the Lord was the most important aspect of his life. His passion was to obey God and carry out His will. However, that doesn't mean he was always obedient. Who can forget his failure with Bathsheba? But even when he sinned by committing adultery and murder, his heart was still focused on God. The conviction he felt and his humble repentance afterward proved that his relationship with the Lord was still his priority.

Could you ask yourself this question; If God is writing a summary of your life, how would He describe you?

WILLINGNESS TO FOLLOW AND OBEY GOD WITH NO QUESTIONS ASKED.

In the book of Genesis 12:1-5 we see a man who was willing to follow God no matter what he was going through; he never had doubts in his heart, he never had a second thought but chose to give himself up whole heartedly in all God commanded him to do. The man was called Abram. Something strange happened to seventy five year old Abram when God, (unknown to him at this point of his life), appeared to him and gave him a 'marching order'. As an adult, he was asked to leave his country, a familiar territory where he was born and raised with all the knowledge of their beliefs, customs, traditions, cultural background and everything he had been brought up to know; to go to an unknown and unfamiliar land with strange customs and way of life. This happened when Abram was 75 years, an age when most in today's world have retired from their jobs or businesses. But in Abram's day, the bible records he was still living with his father even at the age of 75, a strong pointer to the bond he had with his family. But when God called him, he did not hesitate, didn't look behind but said 'YES' Lord I will go. He never questioned God as to where he was going, his accommodation there, provision, 'safe neighbourhood watch', language barrier, climate and all such factors we concern ourselves with today when moving to a new location. In Verse 4, it says Abram left, as the Lord had told him.

Abram had a passion for God. In his heart, God was undoubtedly number one and this made him do whatever God asked him to do without questioning God. Little wonder the bible describes him as "the friend of God" and the father of faith. His name has been engraved in the hall of fame as a man of faith. It had to be nothing other than faith for Abram to do all this; how many of us today as believers can follow in the same footstep? To have such a passion for God that when He calls us to do something, or go somewhere all we ever say, is "Yes Lord" without questioning him. "And I heard the voice of the Lord, saying: "whom shall I send. And who will go for us?" Then I said, "Here am I! Send me,"" {Isaiah 6:8}. Many times God has been beckoning at us, yet we fail to respond. We are more concerned with Him providing answers to our numerous questions on His assignment before we consider if it's worthwhile to go or not. Do we truly have a passion for God as evidenced in Abram's example? Are we willing to follow and obey God with no questions asked like Abraham?

WILLINGNESS TO DIE TO SELF AND LIVE FOR GOD WITH NO CONSIDERATIONS:

If you study church history, you read of Christians who gave up their lives and were butchered because of their love and passion for God. Peter the Apostle was crucified upside down; his head was cut off with a saw. He died rejoicing in the Lord despite the terrible pain. The famous Apostle Paul was also beheaded. Many bold men have sacrificed their lives for the sake of the gospel. In Acts 7, we read about one of the greatest preachers, Stephen being stoned to death after preaching one of the greatest sermons in the Bible. He had the zeal, the driving force and the love of what he was speaking about. But see what happened to him in Acts 7:54-60, we see the stoning of the greatest preacher and the first martyr of the church. Stephen had such a zeal for the Lord to the extent that even summoned before the Sanhedrin council; he wasn't moved but was bold to speak about the risen Lord Jesus Christ. He counted his life a loss and was willing to give all up for the sake of Jesus whom he preached. How many of us will do what Stephen did today? This unquestionably takes passion for God. Paul says in Galatians 2:20 that "I am crucified with Christ; nevertheless I live; yet not I but Christ liveth in me, and the life which I now live in the flesh I live by the faith of the Son of God, who loved me, and gave himself for me."

Before any seed can grow, it has to die first and get buried in the ground in order to have life again. To grow in Christ, we have to give up what we treasure, die with him in order to live for him. Are we willing to die and live for God with no considerations?

There are those who have a passion for God but no willingness. They don't go to church to worship together with brethren where they can manifest the gift of God in their lives. They are saddled with lots of excuses as to why they don't worship.

What did King David's passion do for him?

1 Samuel 17:26-29:

²⁶ And David spake to the men that stood by him, saying, What shall be done to the man that killeth this Philistine, and taketh away the reproach from Israel? for who is this uncircumcised Philistine, that he should defy the armies of the living God?

²⁷ And the people answered him after this manner, saying, So shall it be done to the man that killeth him.

²⁸ And Eliab his eldest brother heard when he spake unto the men; and Eliab's anger was kindled against David, and he said, Why camest thou down

hither? and with whom hast thou left those few sheep in the wilderness? I know thy pride, and the naughtiness of thine heart; for thou art come down that thou mightest see the battle.

²⁹ And David said, What have I now done? Is there not a cause?

His passion motivated him to do the things he loves. It gives him a sense of purpose. It gives him the feeling that he is meant to do great things in life. Despite the circumstances happing on his way, his passion gives him a reason to learn and work toward his goal.

A man with passion never gives up despite how many times he fails.

The army of Israel was at war against the Philistines, but they were intimated by a giant Goliath, standing over 9 feet tall. For 40 days this Philistine came forward every morning and evening and took his stand mocking the people of Israel and their God.

David came to the battle front and got to know what was happening. He came to see his older brothers and bring them food as instructed by his father Jesse.

He heard everything. And he was angry. 17:26 "Who is this uncircumcised Philistine that he should defy the armies of the living God?"

There was this great unease in his heart. How can we let him, come out day after day, and mocks God's army?

He told King Saul when he was brought before him: "Let no one lose heart on account of this Philistine; your servant will go and fight him." (17:32)

17:36 "Your servant has killed both the lion and the bear (when they came to harass my father's sheep); this uncircumcised Philistine will be like one of them, because he has defied the armies of the living God."

Finally when he faced the giant, this was what he said (17:45): "You come against me with sword and spear and javelin, but I come against you in the name of the Lord Almighty, the God of the armies of Israel, whom you have defied."

Something was driving David. Something in him was motivating him that we did not see in the soldiers, who were "dismayed and terrified" (17:11).

David was passionate for God's glory. That motivates him and gives him courage.

God always be glad when He sees your passion corresponds with His desire; No wonder the Lord described him as "a man after my own heart; he will do everything I wanted him to do." (cf. Acts 13:22)

David was driven by a desire to see that God's Name be exalted and God be glorified.

And God will surely glorify Himself through the person who is passionate for His glory.

Not everyone shares the same passion. In fact, his oldest brother Eliab came to him, burning with anger and asked: "Why have you come down here? ... I know how conceited you are and how wicked your heart is; you came down only to watch the battle." (17:28)

God saw a heart after his own heart. Man sees something else, coloured by his own prejudice, jealousy, and pride.

Eliab was more concerned about David's words, than Goliath's mockery of Jehovah's God. David words exposed their cowardice and weakness; their fears.

In life the storm of this world will fight your passion. It was David's passion that leads him to his greatness.

He lives for God's glory. He was quick to repent when he sinned; he was willing to confess when he failed.

HINTS ON PASSION:

"Without passion man is a mere latent force and possibility, like the flint which awaits the shock of the iron before it can give forth its spark." - Henri Frederic Amiel

"Passion is universal humanity. Without it religion, history, romance and art would be useless." - Honore De Balzac

"What is passion? It is surely the becoming of a person. Are we not, for most of our lives, marking time? Most of our being is at rest, unlived. In passion, the body and the spirit seek expression outside of self. Passion is all that is other from self. Sex is only interesting when it releases passion. The more extreme and the more expressed that passion is, the more unbearable does life seem without it. It reminds us that if passion dies or is denied, we are partly dead and that soon, come what may, we will be wholly so." - John Boorman

"Passion doesn't look beyond the moment of its existence." - Christian Nevell Bovee

"Moral passion without entertainment is propaganda, and entertainment without moral passion is television." - Rita Mae Brown

"Men live by intervals of reason under the sovereignty of humor and passion." - Sir Thomas Browne

"Only passions, great passions can elevate the soul to great things." - Denis Diderot

"There is only one passion, the passion for happiness." - Denis Diderot

"Our passions do not live apart in locked chambers but dress in their small wardrobe of notions, bring their provisions to a common table and mess together, feeding out of the common store according to their appetite." - George Eliot

"It is the passions that do and undo everything." - Bernard Le Bovier Fontenelle

"A man in passion rides a horse that runs away with him." - Thomas Fuller

"Passions are vices or virtues to their highest powers." - Johann Wolfgang Von Goethe

"We may affirm absolutely that nothing great in the world has ever been accomplished without passion." - Georg Hegel

"He who has no passion has no principal or motive to act." - Claude A. Helvetius

"What our age lacks is not reflection, but passion." - Soren Kierkegaard

"If we resist our passions, it is more through their weakness than from our strength." - Francois De La Rochefoucauld

"The passions are the only orators which always persuade." - Francois De La Rochefoucauld

"None, but people of strong passion are capable of rising to greatness." - Gabriel Riqueti Mirabeau

"Passion makes the best observations and the sorriest conclusions." - Jean Paul

"The ruling passion, be it what it will, The ruling passion conquers reason still." - Alexander Pope

"I'm very determined and stubborn. There's a desire in me that makes me want to do more and more, and to do it right. Each one of us has a fire in our heart for something. It's our goal in life to find it and to keep it lit." - Mary Lou Retton

"Live with passion!" - Anthony Robbins

"Three passions simple but overwhelmingly strong, have governed my life; the longing for love, the search for knowledge, and unbearable pity for the suffering of mankind." - Bertrand Russell

"Our passions are the winds that propel our vessel. Our reason is the pilot that steers her. Without winds the vessel would not move and without a pilot she would be lost." - Saying

"Passion is in all great searches and is necessary to all creative endeavors." - Eugene W. Smith

"Passion is the drunkenness of the mind." - Bishop Robert South

"Passion is the trigger of success." - Source Unknown

"Chase your passion, not your pension." - Denis Waitley

"I always tried to make clear that basketball is not the ultimate. It is of small importance in comparison to the total life we live. There is only one kind of life that truly wins, and that is the one that places faith in the hands of the Savior. Until that is done, we are on an aimless course that runs in circles and goes nowhere." - John Wooden

"Limitations live only in our minds. But if we use our imaginations, our possibilities become limitless."

~ Jamie Paolinetti quote

"Be yourself. Above all, let who you are, what you are, what you believe, shine through every sentence you write, every piece you finish."

~ John Jakes quotes

"Nothing great in the world has ever been accomplished without passion."

~ Hebbel quotes

"A great leader's courage to fulfill his vision comes from passion, not position."

~ John Maxwell quotes

"The way you get meaning into your life is to devote yourself to loving others, devote yourself to your community around you, and devote yourself to creating something that gives you purpose and meaning."

~ Mitch Albom quotes

"The more intensely we feel about an idea or a goal, the more assuredly the idea, buried deep in our subconscious, will direct us along the path to its fulfillment."

~ Earl Nightingale quotes

YOU NEED FAITH TO ERECT AN ALTAR, Heb.11; 6.

We need to roll the dice again and examine the cause of our frustrations. Let us get to the foundation of the matter. The word of God says that without faith you cannot please God. God is the author of faith and is a God of Faith. In the beginning He spoke things in existence before they materialized in the physical. If we're to approach and understand God, we need to approach Him in faith; faith is the user name and password for pleasing Him. Unfortunately, faith cannot be bought. It comes only by hearing the Word of GOD. Faith is what we all need to possess "Having passion and the willingness for God". You can read Christian books; attend church services but when you have no passion for God, it becomes a religion to you, an obligation you have to fulfill without caring about outcomes.

Faith empowers us to build a divine altar of worship of hope and expectation for the bright future of our children. You can't invest in anything you consider trustworthy without having faith in it. "Now faith is the substance of things hoped for, the evidence of things not seen," {Hebrews 11:1}. Faith is the ability to look beyond the visible into the invisible. It is the ability to look beyond the momentary temporal scene fixing your focus on what you know to be true. As we focus on what we know to be true, we are empowered by faith to live in harmony with that truth. The truth we speak of is the eternal truth of God. So it takes faith to have an altar of truth.

Faith is impossible without a proper viewpoint, and eternal truth is designed to give us a proper perception in worshipping God. Colossians 1:9.

The psalmist's understanding of God's everlasting reliability gives him assurance and confidence to maintain his faith in a temporary world. Faith in God gives us the advantage to view our lives from the certainty of God's eternal perspective. Faith allows us to live in view of eternity and live from the perspective of eternity. Faith allows us to see our lives from God's benefit point. The Hebrew writer tells us that only faith in God will give us a proper perspective from which we can view the present. Faith sharpens our vision. Abraham was able to look beyond his tents to a city whose builder and maker was God.

An altar of faith increases familiarity and growth in intimacy with God. We must be committed to growth no matter how long we have been saved.

Abraham came to know God more than what the god of his father could offer him. Due to his hunger for God, he cultivated a deeper intimacy with God.

Receiving God's promises and having His power to overcome the enemy is desirable, but is not a replacement for growing in intimacy with God on a personal level.

Abraham's faith was not derived from a system; rather it was developed through relationship on a personal level. An intimate walk with God will produce an impacting work among men. The Lord wants to work in, and with, for and through yielded vessels. When you build an altar, you invite God in and He dwells in a place of sacrifice; a place of worship, and a place of prayer.

Every Christian altar of worship is built by faith and carries the undeniable presence of God.

FAITH NECESSITATES DILIGENCE:

The Hebrews lacked diligence. A lack of diligence led to ignorance and unbelief resulting in lack of perseverance. The writer reminds them that God only rewards earnest seekers.

"But without faith it is impossible to please Him, for he who comes to God must believe that He is, and that He is a rewarder of those who diligently seek Him," {Hebrews 11:6}.

According to the writer of the book of Hebrew, our faith in God informs how we live in the present. The Bible makes it abundantly clear that it is impossible for God to initiate his plan of grace in our life until we seek him through responsive faith.

"By faith Abel offered to God a more excellent sacrifice than Cain, through which he obtained witness that he was righteous, God testifying of his gifts; and through it he being dead still speaks. By faith Enoch was taken away so that he did not see death, "and was not found, because God had taken him"; for before he was taken he had this testimony, that he pleased God," {Hebrews 11:4-5}.

Abel's faith resulted in offerings; his offerings spoke well of him. Enoch's faith and living style pleased God. Noah's faith motivated him to build an ark when warned of God. Abraham's faith moved him to wait on the promised seed-son. Abraham's faith moved him to offer the promised son as a sacrifice. By faith Jacob blessed his sons before he died. By faith Moses' parents hid Moses because they trusted God. By faith the Israelites passed through the Red Sea. By faith the walls of Jericho fell after the Israelites marched around them for seven days. By faith Rahab hid the spies.

There is not one instance in this entire chapter that suggest that God's graceful plan for their lives didn't require faith that moved them to obey God. More importantly, without their obedience to God's plan there would be no salvation for us today. The grace, which came through Jesus Christ, was predicated upon their assurance and manifested in their obedience.

Their assurance allowed God to work out his plan through their confident obedience. God's plan for each of their lives had to be acted on by faith.

God's work where he led the Hebrews through the wilderness for forty years was well known by surrounding nations and this instilled fear in their hearts concerning the Hebrew people. A clear example of this is what the prostitute told the Hebrew spies whom she helped house, the perception held by the people of Jericho about the Hebrew people on getting to know about their planned invasion of Jericho. "And before they lay down, she came up to them on the roof, and said to the men: I know that the LORD has given you the land, that the terror of you has fallen on us, and that all the inhabitants of the land are fainthearted because of you. "For we have heard how the LORD dried up the water of the Egypt, and what you did to the two kings of the Amorites who were on the other side of the Jordan, Sihon and Og whom you utterly destroyed. And as soon as we heard these things, our hearts melted; neither did there remain any more courage in anyone because of you, for the LORD your God, He is God in heaven above and on earth beneath," {Joshua 2:9-11}.

FAITH MUST CONQUER OUR FEARS

One of the most important promises God gives us to counter such fear is in Isaiah 41:10. It says, "Fear thou not; for I am with thee; be not dismayed; for I am thy God. I will strengthen thee; yea, I will uphold thee with the right hand of my righteousness."

Jesus wasn't talking about our saving faith, but our daily living faith. Our daily living faith rises and falls according to the strength of our relationship with God. When we are not in constant intimacy with God, the first storm that hits us will create fear and panic in our hearts.

Faith that conquers fear depends on absolute trust in God. It is the kind of faith that has an open heart to God's plan for us. It is a faith that is manifested as an utter dependence on the sovereignty of God. When we live by faith, we know that even when the storm is at its worst, we can trust that God is working out His purposes for us.

When Jesus rebuked the disciples for their lack of faith, He was referring to their failure to trust Him in this practical situation. How often do we trust God with our hearts, yet not our daily needs? God wants us to trust Him not only with our salvation, but also with our relationships, our resources, and our future. He wants to see our professed faith in action. He wants us to put our complete trust in Him for every detail of our lives.

When we walk close with God and trust Him daily, our faith will conquer our fears. When we put our focus on God, fear fades into the background. At the first sign of fear, our plan of action should be seeking God in prayer.

"By faith the harlot Rahab perished not with them that believed not, when she had received the spies with peace. And what shall I more say? For the time would fall me to tell of Gedeon, and of Barak, and of Samson, and of Jephthae; of David also, and Samuel, and of the prophets: Who through faith subdued kingdoms, wrought righteousness, obtained promises, stopped the mouths of Lions. Quenched the violence of fire, escaped the edge of the sword, out of weakness were made strong, waxed valiant in fight, turned to flight the armies of the aliens. Woman received their dead raised to life again: and others were tortured, not accepting deliverance; that they might obtain a better resurrection: And others had trial of cruel mocking and scourging, yea, moreover of bonds and imprisonment: They were stoned, they were sawn asunder, were tempted, were slain with the sword: they wandered about in sheepskins and goatskins; being destitute, afflicted, tormented; (of whom the world was not worthy:) they wandered in deserts, and in mountains, and in dens and caves of the earth. And these all, having obtained a good report through faith, received not the promise; God having provided some better thing for us, that they without us should not be made perfect," {Hebrews 11:31-40}.

These verses talks about great men and women of faith that courageously struggled to maintain their personal faith in God when all the odds were against them.

RAHAB THE PROSTITUTE'S FAITH IS AMAZING:

The book of Joshua introduces us to one of the most amazing and thought provoking women of the Old Testament. Rehab the prostitute earned unique praise for her faith, and a place in the lineage of Christ. Certainly the faith this woman revealed demonstrates the potential we all have; yet she also reminds us to not judge--how many of us would expect a great act of faith from a hooker? How many of us would rather have crossed over to the other-side of the street when walking along the street she lived on to avoid being contaminated? Yet God blessed this woman beyond measure because of her act of faith towards the spies by including her in the lineage of Christ. God's blessings come upon the least expected.

GOD ROUTED 10,000 PHILISTINES WITH GIDEON'S 300 MEN:

God dealt Gideon a blow of shock when God told him: "Gideon, you still has too many men to fight the Midianites. Take your remaining men down to the water and let them drink. There's more sorting to do, and those I select will go for the battle. But the rest, like those before them, should also return home" {Judges 7:4}.

Ten thousand Israelites welcomed a cool, refreshing drink of water. The overwhelming majority-9,700-got down on their knees, placed their mouths to the water and drank. A peculiar destined 300 crouched and scooped the water to their mouths with their hands to drink. These 300 God said would make up his army {Judges7: 4-8}. God hand-picked Gideon's army; 300 men whose distinct characteristic was not in proving themselves as mighty men of valour, but choosing to drink water from a position different from the others.

From 32,000 to 300, Gideon's army became only a fraction of what it had been. Surely God knew what He was doing? Gideon might have wondered if they wouldn't have been better off going home. Had God forgotten that Gideon's little band of soldiers would face an experienced army outnumbering them 450 to 1? From all appearances, this situation made no sense.

God explained to Gideon His purpose for allowing him such a small army to battle the physically and numerically superior Midianites. He was not going to allow Israel to boast that her own strength had saved her {Judges7:2; 1 Corinthians 1:27-29}. That honour would go to God alone. But God would work through Gideon.

BARAK IN JUDGES 4-5:

We take a look at Barak in the book of Judges. Barak asked Deborah to come with him to battle. Deborah going with Barak helps him to conquer his fear of losing in battle. Why would a man ask a woman to come along with him in a battle simply because Deborah had a tangible and visible relationship with God which was apparent to Barak. Your relationship with God is an important weapon faith used to conquer fear. Barak and all who went with him against Sisera and his army showed real courage and trust in God. They had essentially no weapons to fight with against a technologically advanced army {having 900 chariots of iron}, and God led them to fight on a plain, putting them at a big disadvantage.

THE STORY OF SAMSON

Samson is a historical figure but he is an example of today's typical Christian. All Christians have the indwelling Holy Spirit, who empowers us to do all that God wants us to do, especially to deliver His people from Satan's hold. "But ye are not in the flesh, but in the Spirit, if so be that the Spirit of God dwell in you. Now if any man has not the Spirit of Christ, he is none of his," {Romans 8:9}.

Samson's strength was not from his physique, training or diet. His strength was not of him but of the Holy Spirit of God. In other words, he was an ordinary man who had the infinite resources of the indwelling God. Though he was an Old Testament child of God, he had the power of a New Testament Christian!

He defeated a lion, which can be use to symbolize Satan, in his God given strength. The bible declares "Be sober, be vigilant; because your adversary the devil, as a roaring lion, walketh about, seeking whom he may devour,"

{1Peter 5:8}. Sampson also used his strength to kill 1000 Philistines, who symbolize God's enemies and also to remove a huge city gate, which symbolizes an undefeatable obstacle.

JEPHTHAH:

The Israelites needed a leader to help them defeat the Ammonites, but didn't seem to have a candidate for the job. In their desperation, they vowed that whoever would lead them to victory, they would make that man head of all the inhabitants.

Jephthah "was a valiant warrior" but he was not considered for the job of a leader because of his background. His father was Gilead but his mother a harlot; no right thinking person identifies with harlot in any manner. Even though he had no choice in choosing his mother, Jephthah was rejected because of his mother. His step-mom and his half brothers looked down on him and treated him cruelly. His step-brothers told him, "You shall not have an inheritance in our father's house, for you are the son of another woman." Thus, Jephthah was driven away, not only from his father's house but from the entire homeland.

Undoubtedly, Jephthah had a painful childhood because of this rejection. It is not wrong to expect that your family of birth ought to love and accept you unconditionally even if no one else does. To be rejected by one's family is one of the most painful things anyone can experience. I believe Jephthah felt worthless.

One of the reasons why Jephthah became "a valiant warrior" was that he determined by faith to survive in a cruel world. In order to survive in the world, you will have to build up your faith in God to toughen you up and see you through the numerous challenges which come your way in your day-to-day living.

We realize that God removed the impossibilities from the lives of these people. However, it is evident that he could not have done this without their courageous personal faith in him. It was God who shut the mouths of lions for Daniel, but Daniel's personal faith that made it possible.

All these individuals conquered their fears by faith as they looked up to God to see them through the hurdles of life. Faith in God helped them to conquer their worst fears and enabled them triumph over difficulties. Can you imagine Moses' parents considering the options available to them in trying to save their son from Pharaoh's destruction order; the one son who eventually would save the Hebrew people from bondage?

Fear is the most common negative emotion in the universe. It wastes away our physical, mental energy, and spiritual ability. It is a stumbling block to any type of progress; both physical and spiritual. The origin, type and intensity of fear vary from person to person. Notwithstanding, fear haunts us all. It is a great shame that despite our inherent divinity, we continue to be held hostage by fear.

Fear keeps us in constant state of agitation and turmoil. Fear gives birth to mental weakness which results in constant stress and strain. It brings misery and misfortune. Weakness emanating from fear makes us live life under delusion. Delusion limits us to the body-mind complex. Deceived, we continue to suffer in the cauldron of fear and weakness. The moment a person becomes aware of his true divine nature it instantly dawns on him that there is nothing in this world to be afraid of. Fearlessness is very much within our reach provided we make a strong determination to lift off the cap of ignorance.

Faith is a spiritual component that each person has to develop on their own. Be assured, God has made a way for you to be free once and for all from the torment of fear. God has indeed given you the faith to overcome your fear and live above it forever. "And when they had sent away the multitude, they took him even as he was in the ship. And there were also with him other little ships. And there arose a great storm of wind, and the waves beat into the ship, so that it was now full. And he was in the hinder part of the ship, asleep on a pillow: and they awake him, and say unto him, Master, carest thou not that we perish? And he arose, and rebuked the wind, and said unto the sea, Peace, be still. And the wind ceased, and there was a great calm. And he said unto them, why are ye so fearful? How is it that ye have no faith?" {Mark 4:36-40}.

I want you to picture this scene in your mind. Jesus and His disciples were crossing the Sea of Galilee. Jesus was asleep in the bottom of the boat. Suddenly, the wind began to blow and the waves began to rise. As water began flooding the boat, the disciples became fearful. They forgot that Jesus the Master of the wind and waves was on board with them. Then someone remembered that He was asleep below. They rushed down, shook Him and Jesus awoke. They said, "Jesus, the wind is whipping the boat, and water is flooding the bow. We're about to go under! Don't you even care that we're about to perish?" Jesus got up and went to the bow of the boat. He stretched out His hands and said, "Peace, be still." He hushed the sea to sleep with the authority of His Word and then turned to His disciples and said, "why are ye so fearful? How is it that ye have no faith?"

My friend, I believe that Jesus is still asking us that same question today; "where is your Faith?" When faced with seemingly insurmountable challenges, we forget who we are in Christ, act like the disciples of old and cower because of fear. We become frightened and alarmed at the storms around us when Jesus is actually beside us saying, "Your faith will overcome your fear."

There are four actions you can take to overcome your fear and replace it with faith. If you accept and practice them, you won't be the same again. This faith over fear formula will help you live triumphantly in the face of storms. The first action is:

1. ACKNOWLEDGE THAT TORMENTING FEAR IS NOT FROM GOD:

The Bible mentions two types of fear. The first type is beneficial and to be encouraged; the second is detrimental and needs to be overcome. The first type is fear of the Lord. This type of fear does not necessarily mean to be afraid of something. Rather, it is a reverential fear of God; a reverence for His person, power and glory. It is also an appropriate respect for His wrath and anger. In other words, the fear of the Lord is a total acknowledgement of God; having a profound knowledge of Him and His attributes.

The fear of the Lord brings with it many blessings and benefits. It is the beginning of wisdom and leads to good understanding {Psalm 111:10}. Only fools despise wisdom and discipline {Proverbs 1:7}. Furthermore, fear of the Lord leads to life, rest, peace, and contentment {Proverbs 19:23}. It is the fountain of life {Proverbs 14:27} and provides a security and a place of safety for us {Proverbs 14:26}. Based on the definition, this fear of God is to be encouraged for all to practice.

However, the second type of fear mentioned in the Bible is not beneficial at all. This is the "spirit of fear" mentioned in 2 Timothy 1:7 "For God hath not given us the spirit of fear; but of power, and of love, and of a sound mind." A spirit of fearfulness and timidity does not come from God.

Sometimes we become afraid because the "spirit of fear" seizes or overcomes us. To overcome it, we need to trust in and love God completely. "There is no fear in love. But perfect love drives out fear, because fear has to do with punishment. The one who fears is not made perfect in love" {1 John 4:18}. No one is perfect, and God knows this and is the reason God has liberally encouraged against fear in various passages in the Bible. From the book of Genesis right through to the book of Revelation God dutifully reminds us to "Fear not".

For example, Isaiah 41:10 encourages, "Fear thou not; for I am with thee; be not dismayed; for I am thy God. I will strengthen thee; yea, I will uphold thee with the right hand of my righteousness." Often we are afraid of what will become of us in the future. Jesus reminds us that if God cares for the birds of the air, how much more will He provide for His children? "So don't be afraid; you are worth more than many sparrows" {Matthew 10:31}. Just these few verses cover many different types of fear. God tells us not to be afraid of being alone, of being too weak, of not being heard, and of lacking necessities. These admonishments continue throughout the Bible, covering the many different aspects of the "spirit of fear."

In Psalm 56:11 the psalmist writes, "In God have I put my trust: I will not be afraid what man can do to me." This is an awesome testimony to the power of trusting in God. Notwithstanding of what happens, the psalmist trusts in God because he knows and understands the power of God. The key to overcoming fear, then, is total and complete trust in God. Trusting God is a refusal to give in to fear. It is a turning to God even in the darkest times and trusting Him to make things right. This trust comes from knowing God and knowing that He is good. As Job said when he was experiencing some of the most difficult trials recorded in the Bible, "Though he slay me, yet will I trust in him...." {Job 13:15}.

Once we have learned to put our trust in God, we will no longer be afraid of the things that come against us. We will be like the psalmist who said with confidence "But let all those that put their trust in thee rejoice: let them ever shout for joy, because thou defendest them: let them also that love thy name be joyful in thee," {Psalm 5:11}.

2.   REMEMBER WHAT JESUS DID FOR YOU

"There is therefore now no condemnation to them which are in Christ Jesus, who walk not after the flesh, but after the Spirit. For the law of the Spirit of life in Christ Jesus hath made me free from the law of sin and death", {Romans 8:1-2}.

The crucifixion and resurrection of Jesus Christ are not mere symbolic representations but actual events. What Jesus did almost 2,000 years ago was the most courageous, loving and agonizing action ever taken by man. It was courageous because Jesus willingly took the wrath of God upon himself to pay for the ugliness and wickedness of sin. He knew full well what would happen to Him; He knew the pain he would endure and yet He took this punishment willingly, courageously. His action is a loving one as he put others before Himself. He died so that humanity would live. This was the most selfless act in all of history. His death was regarded as violent because he destroyed the power of the kingdom of darkness and of death. Death lost its sting, the grave its victory!

Sin is a destructive act. It condemns and takes away your happiness in life and tears you down. God doesn't want you to go through life with a load of sin. That's why he sent Jesus Christ to set you free. Jesus won the victory for you through his death and resurrection, so if you want to live a life free of sin, you need to remind yourself daily of what Jesus did for you.

Romans 8:1 say, "There is therefore now no condemnation to them which are in Christ Jesus, who walk not after the flesh, but after the Spirit". If you are a believer, have accepted Jesus as your Lord and Savior and are walking after the Spirit of God, you are not condemned. This doesn't mean that once you become a Christian you no longer sin or make mistakes. You will. But when you confess your sins, you will be forgiven because you are no longer in condemnation; you are no longer judged. You are free from the consequences of sin because Jesus took the condemnation on your behalf on the cross.

Remembering what Jesus did for you also gives you a new power greater than willpower. Will power only lasts a few weeks or months before you finally give up and go back to your old habits and temptations. But "For the law of the Spirit of life in Christ Jesus hath made me free from the law of sin and death", {Romans 8:2}.

There are a lot of self-help plans out there to help you change, and together with your willpower, you may succeed at the plan for a few weeks. Your own efforts can only go so far. Knowing the right thing to do doesn't mean you have the power to do it. Lasting change will only come when your inner nature changes. The only way to change your sinful inner nature is to accept the power of God's life-giving Spirit into your life through His Son Jesus Christ. God's plan for lasting change is this: "For what the law could not do, in that it was weak through the flesh, God sending his own Son in the likeness of sinful flesh, and for sin, condemned sin the flesh: That the righteousness of the law might be fulfilled in us, who walk not after the flesh, but after the Spirit," {Romans 8:3-4}.

In **Mark, chapter 5**, the Bible tells us about a man the devil tried unsuccessfully to torment with fear. One day Jesus was walking down a road and was surrounded by a crowd. A man named Jairus, who was a ruler in the synagogue, walked up to Him and fell down at His feet to worship. He asked Jesus to come to his house and heal his little daughter who was near death. Jesus, seeing the need in the man's life, went with him. On the way there, one of Jairus' servants came and said, "Jairus, you don't need to trouble Jesus anymore. Your daughter is dead!"

Can you imagine the look on Jairus' face? His hope for a possible intervention in his daughter's case was gone and anxiety, fear and torment took hold of him.

Jesus looked at Jairus and said, "Fear not, believe only." In other words, "Jairus, you don't need to be afraid. I'm right here with you so you just keep on believing." And when Jesus arrived at the house He brought healing to the little girl and restored her life.

What ever it is you're going through, Jesus is saying the exact same words to you right now. "Don't be afraid of the situation you see. Don't be afraid of what you see, hear or think. Keep on believing because I'm beside you with all of my power."

Be rests assured; no matter what the devil is trying around you, Jesus is always by your side. He will never leave you {Matthew 28:20}. He is always with you to help you overcome your fear and to encourage you in your faith.

It is important to grasp this truth if you are desire to replace your fear with faith.

a.   **KNOW THAT YOU ALREADY HAVE FAITH**

Did you know that you have faith? The Bible says in Romans 12:3 that "God hath dealt to every man the measure of faith." You are no exception! You make use your faith every day, in almost everything you do, even in something as simple as wearing shoes. You have faith that the shoes you wear is designed in a way that will support your frame and provide comfort without your feet being injured. If you did not have faith in them to deliver, you would not have worn them at all.

It is not so much of how much faith you have but what you do with the level of faith you have. You can have all the faith in the world, but if you don't do something with it, your faith won't do you any good. That is why it is important that you need to take the fourth action to overcome your fear with faith:

Some brethren doubt that they do have faith. Sometimes they feel like they are merely acting out a role. The only thing clear to them is that they want to believe. Romans 10:9-10 "That if thou shalt confess with thy mouth the Lord Jesus, and shalt believe in thine heart that God halt raised him from the dead, thou shalt be saved. For with the heart man believeth unto righteousness; and with the mouth confession is made unto salvation".

Now if you have done that it means you have faith because faith is an act not a feeling. The moment you accepted Jesus into your heart faith came into. You have faith. According to the book of Romans 12:3 that says, "For i say, through the grace given unto me, to every man that is among you, not to think of himself more highly than he ought to think soberly, according as God hath dealt to every man the measure of faith". This means that anyone who was or has been born again has the same level of faith. You now need to nurture your faith. Recognize the fact you are a real believer because you accepted the Lord Jesus into your life and with this acceptance came faith which needs to be nurtured by you. Faith is an act of what you believe in and therefore cannot be faked. Faith is taking action because of a hope in something. Often the Saviour asks of us to do certain things or live in certain ways as recorded in Genesis 12. When we see a stranger in distress, we stop and help them as Jesus commanded us to just like the Good Samaritan in Luke 10:25. The act of helping is the evidence of our Faith in Christ. We are asked to tithe. Tithing is evidence of our faith. We tithe in hopes of the promises in Malachi 3:10 that the floodgates of Heaven are open to us.

Faith is when we put our beliefs and hope into action.

As Christians, the bible tells us in 2 Corinthians 5:7 that "we walk by faith not by sight" this means we don't live and act according to our feelings but we live according to the Word of God.

b.   **FAITH IS ACTIVATED WHEN WE ACT**

Faith isn't just something you talk about; it's something you *do*. Faith is only activated when we act. We have faith in God when we do what he says.

We can come to church every weekend and listen to the word of God preached and feel very spiritual as a result. If one does that, they're like one who goes to a health club and watches people exercise without participating. Not taking part in the exercises does not make one healthy. Reading and listening to God's Word without acting on it won't make you more spiritual either. You're fooling yourself if you think it will. It's not just enough to say that you agree with what God's Word says on a subject; you must act on it. God's word is meant to be acted upon. God wants us to apply the word 100 Percent in principle. Obey God 100 percent of the time in all aspects of your life. You can't be 100 percent obedient in just 80 percent of your life; it's not a complete faith walk.

"Not forsaking the assembling of ourselves together, as the manner of some is; but exhorting one another: and so much the more, as ye see the day approaching" - Hebrews 10:25.

Something important we need to understand here is this; "As the body without the spirit is dead, so faith without actions is dead".

We can easily activate our faith when we gather together, hear the word of God, encourage ourselves by getting involved with others and sharing testimonies on God's deed in our lives. We can_activate our faith by recognizing, committing, and responding to the word of God according to our commitment.

Some of the reasons why Christians defect from God's service and absent themselves from worship are that they are engaged in business. Some are too busy to meet regularly with the brethren to worship and praise God and remember the sacrifice of His Son. Others may say, they have to attend their village meeting and that is why they can't fellowship. While some sisters claim they are preparing dinner for their children. Some brothers are engaged in the pursuit of their business. Is this faithfulness? Is this true

Christianity? With such people, Christianity is on the side line. I believe that a Christian who forsakes the assembly of the brethren to attend to their personal business is yet to have a personal encounter with Jesus Christ.

It is important to know that there is a unique peculiarity about each gathering we have, something done or said that will never be repeated in the same manner and under the same circumstances. Only those present at the time will partake of the blessing.

Both the inward and the outward must go hand-in-hand for a complete picture. The assembling together of saints is commanded and has to be fulfilled by each saint. Forsaking the gathering of the assembly is a dangerous symptom of backsliding. They are reminded not only to be faithful in their walk with the Lord, but also to care for others. They are charged to exhort one another for exercising and strengthening their faith; for hope, for love to which we have been urged for complete development of life in the Holiest of All. In addition, they are charged to help and comfort all who are feeble; to cultivate the fellowship of the Spirit and the Word; the assembling together of ourselves has unspeakable value.

Hebrews 11 speaks about faith. It proves that it is both action and belief and these are some people that activated their faith through action.

i. "By faith Abel offered unto God a more excellent sacrifice than Cain, by which he obtained witness that he was righteous." {Hebrew 11:4}.

In Genesis 4 Abel offered the best he had to give because he believed in and was responding to his provider. This shows both his belief and active response.

ii. "By faith Enoch was translated… without faith it is impossible to please him: for he that cometh to God must believe that he is, and that he is a rewarder of them that diligently seek him." {Hebrews 11:5–6}.

Enoch believed in God and He actively responded to Him by seeking Him another act of belief and response.

iii. "By faith Noah, being warned of God of things not seen as yet, moved with fear, prepared an ark to the saving of his house." {Hebrews 11:7}.

Noah believed in God and actively responded by being obedient to God's instructions to build an ark.

iv. I encourage you to go through the over 20 examples given throughout this chapter of faith in Hebrews 11 and see how everyone mentioned as being faithful were people who believed and acted on their belief.

They had a belief that they made known by responding to God in an action pleasing to Him.

If we desire to activate our faith as Christians we need to look closely at the things we dare say we believe.

6

The Benefits of building an Altar

God is a God of benefits and he is ever ready to reward those who offer Him their precious time. It is sin for one not to acknowledge God. Hence, it is up to you to decide whether or not to serve Him.

It allows you the individual or group to have a direct connection with the Lord when you choose to seek Him.

You learn new and creative ways of doing things through His revelation to you in various situations in your life.

Building an altar is a positive way to do something through divine revelation about negative things in your life which are adversely affecting you. The connection with the Lord is always a good thing.

It helps you to have a spiritual center in your life even though you participate in your church activities. However, you can still build your personal altar or family altar. It will still enrich your life.

Building altars is meditative and relaxing.

Building an altar creates a spiritual atmosphere in your home and brings down God's presence into your home.

An altar is another way to introduce children to God and emphasis on the need of worshipping Him in spirit and truth in our physical body through a life of holiness and righteousness.

The benefits are huge in doing this. We are reminding the family that God is there and that God is in charge, that we must go by God's Word and follow God's rules. It's good for instance, for parents to know God never slumbers or sleeps and our children also need to know. How are they going to know this if we don't teach them? Remember, the average young person never reads the Bible. Many adults don't either. These truths must be communicated to the young ones {and the older ones}. This can be done during the family altar meetings.

TO ENCOUNTER AND COMMUNE WITH GOD:

Having recognized the benefit for having a divine altar as a means of identifying yourself with God, using it as a point of encounter with Him; it is from here you develop enduring attitudes essential for growth in any relationship: love, forgiveness, sincerity, kindness, giving, faithfulness, patience, etc, "But the fruit of the Spirit is love, joy, peace, longsuffering, gentleness, goodness, faith, Meekness, temperance: against such there is no law," {Galatians 5:22}.

When we accept Jesus Christ into our lives, we acquire an uncreated life, the divine life of God, which is eternal life. This type of life helps us discipline our human tendencies and fleshly desires. We are able to forgive easily when our partners offend us; we are able to love without conditions; we are able to share willingly the things that we have; and we are able to live in unity despite our differences. These help to build a strong and lasting relationship.

At the altar, God wants to have fellowship with you; hear your voice; commune with you; speak with you as He did to Moses. This second altar symbolizes the place of communion, face to face meeting point with your maker.

One of the benefits for building an altar is that it helps one to commune with God by having a good intimate relationship. The change of heart we experience as Christians results a relationship with God and with others that is marked by supernatural unity.

Worshipping God on your altar is having communion with God. In worship, there is mutual communication and mutual giving and receiving.

Our marriages usually succeed because we develop a satisfying relationship, not because the wedding vows are posted on the refrigerator door. Communion is about relationship, not about fulfilling obligations.

Communion enables someone to explore. Communion also offers great open doors to know God more. The One who made us intends us for himself. Our understanding of him will never wear out. Each new insight files is our appetite to know more. The more we know Him, the more we want to know Him.

ABRAHAM'S THIRD ENCOUNTER: RECONCILIATION WITH GOD

The third time Abraham had an interface at the altar of the living God was when he actually came back to the altar he had built before going down to Egypt. The implication is that Abraham came out of Egypt a very prosperous man but without God and therefore had to return to the last point of contact with God. Does it look like God has abandoned or forgotten you? Go back to the last point of contact or last place of Obedience to God!!! Many use the proof of a new job, status, wealth or circle of friends to measure their accomplishment. But if God seems missing from your life, no amount of material accomplishments can replace Him. Don't ever use your abundant material substance to determine the presence of God. Jesus said, a man's life does not consist or is not measured by the abundance of things he possesses {Lk12:15}. With all that you have, can you confidently declare you have God?

Having encounter with God is an access through which God reveals His purposes unto mankind.

According to www.northoaksbaptist.com

WHAT GOD SAYS ABOUTWORSHIP

Some Lessons About Worship from God's Examples

"We have recognized that God embedded valuable lessons in many examples about worship in His Word. In previous lessons we looked at four of these examples; three which were from the life of Abraham.

The first example: Cain and Abel Genesis 4:1-12

The second example: Abraham and Melchizedek Genesis 14:18-24

The third example: The Pre-incarnate Son of God Visits Abraham Genesis 18:1-15

The fourth example: Abraham offers Isaac as a sacrifice to God Genesis 22:1-17

The fifth example: Joshua assumed his leadership role recognizing that he serves the Lord, received an assurance from the Lord after bowing before Him in worship - Joshua 5:13-6:2

We have already learned the following lessons from these five examples God set before us:

1. God has clearly shown just as there are acceptable ways to approach Him, there are also unacceptable ways to approach Him. He accepts the worship of those who comply with His requirements, but rejects the worship of those who try to approach Him on their terms.

2. God has pointed out if a sinner, (which we all are) desires to approach Him; we must have our sins done away with through atonement by the *"blood-sacrifice"* of Jesus Christ.

3. We can learn from Cain's experience that if our worship of God is unacceptable, we will retain our burden of sin which creates all kinds of problems for us, including alienation from God and from people.

4. From Cain and Abel's (and Adam and Eve's) experience we learn that God is not just a God of love, but also a God of wrath. It reminds us that *"The fear of the Lord is the beginning of knowledge..."* (Proverbs 1:7).

5. Going by Abraham's experience with Melchizedek in Genesis 14, we learn that proper worship of God involves recognizing His ownership of all that is in heaven and on the earth and consequently expressing that recognition by giving Him tithes (10%) of everything we acquire, no matter what that process of acquisition may be.

6. Abraham's experience in Genesis 14 teaches us that God pours out His blessings on those who please Him.

7. The act of Abraham giving a tithe to Melchizedek in front of the king of Sodom coupled with his declaration of dependence upon the *"...Most high God...,"* reveals to us that our tithing and dependence upon God can be a powerful public testimony to unbelievers: *"And Abram said to the king of Sodom, I have lifted up mine hand unto the Lord, the most high God, the possessor of heaven and earth, That I will not take from a thread even to a shoelatchet, and that I will not take any thing that is thine, lest thou shouldest say, I have made Abram rich:"* (Genesis. 14:22-23).

8. Of a certainty God makes promises that He keeps and is truly worthy of our worship.

9. When we try to make God's promises happen, we make a mess of things and cause problems upon us and others.

10. We need to keep our heart in a state of readiness to hear from God by being faithful and obedient at all times. This attitude enables us respond when God chooses to speak to us

11. When and how we worship God and the subsequent release of His blessings upon our lives is solely dependent on Him, not us.

12. In worshipping God, we prostrate, bow (either physically or in attitude) before Him as an act of reverence because of who He is.

13. In our worship to God, we ought to give Him the best that we have.

Some Lessons About Worship from God's Examples

14. God has the right to demand we give back to Him as an act of worship, anything He gave us no matter how precious that gift may have been.

15. God expects us to obey Him in totality no matter how difficult it may be for us to understand or comply with anything He tells us to do. Our obedience is an outward expression of our faith in Him.

16. When we obey God as Abraham did, our children will find joy, peace and confidence to face any obstacle with calm acceptance no matter the challenge facing them.

17. When we offer to God that which is most precious and important to us, we prove to ourselves that we do really have faith in Him, in His directions, and in His provisions.

18. When we give Him back our best, the most valuable and the most precious thing we received from Him, we prove to Him and us that we love Him, the Giver, more than the gift He gave.

19. By worshipping God in this manner, giving the most valuable and the most precious thing we have received from Him, we prove the validity of who we are and our faith in Him, and also become an avenue of blessing to the whole world.

20. The most valuable and precious thing we received from God is ourselves, our being; that is what He wants most from us.

21. When we give back to God in worship the most precious thing He has given to us, we should never forget that God has the resurrection power and is able to bring back to life that which is dead and has lost its life and usefulness.

22. When God calls us to serve Him He always provides whatever we need to be successful. All we need is to be obedient to Him.

23. We are more likely to recognize Him in our obedience, when He presents Himself to us.

24. Whenever we face a daunting challenge and feel we may not overcome, our Lord is always present with us with both His presence, power and every divine resource to enable us achieve victory.

25. In God's presence we are to do two things:

    1) Prostrate before Him in worship.
    2) Ask what His instructions are. Not only did Joshua do this, Paul did this on his conversion (Acts 9:6).

26. We are to respect the holiness of God in our actions. The Lord told Joshua to take his shoes off to visibly and physically show his respect for God's holiness.

27. The Lord chooses how He wishes to appear to any of His servants. The form the Lord used in appearing to Joshua is different from but consistent with His actions in other places and times. See 2 Kings 6:8-18 for another example of the Lord sending His army to protect one of His servants.

28. Men come and go but God abides for ever to accomplish His plans and purposes through those whom He chooses. God will always find a man with a willing heart and enable him to do wonderful things to bring glory to God. See Joshua 1:1-2 and 2:9-12.

29. What God did yesterday He can do again today. He dried up the Red Sea for the Israelites when they left Egypt and dried up the flooded Jordan River when the Israelites entered the promised land.

God's continuity is not affected by the changing variables of this world.

Some Lessons About Worship from God's Examples

30. Your heart should be in a state preparedness at all times to hearken to God if called to serve Him to accomplish the impossible; example the defeat of Jericho. You prepare your heart by worshiping Him reverencing, respecting and utterly depending on Him and His will.

Such people access the powerful and unlimited resources of heaven to overcome the difficulties of life in this world.

THE SIXTH EXAMPLE: David refuses to offer a sacrifice to the Lord that *"cost him nothing."* 1 Chronicles 21:1- 30; 2 Samuel 24:1-25

We now focus on David's attempt to offer a sacrifice to the Lord as part of his repentance for his sin. There are two accounts of this event. Since the reference in 1 Chronicles is from the official "chronicler" of the history of Israel and includes a bit more information, it will serve as our primary reference. We may use a quote or two from the reference in 2 Samuel for further clarification. The event we are studying is described in 1 Chronicles 21:18-30 but in order to have better understanding on the subject matter it is necessary for us to consider the preceding events that gave rise to our focus.

BACKGROUND AND SETTING:

1 Chronicles 21:1-2 *And Satan stood up against Israel, and provoked David to number Israel. And David said to Joab and to the rulers of the people, Go, number Israel from Beer-sheba even to Dan; and bring the number of them to me, that I may know it.*

WHAT HAPPENED?

In his old age David decided that he wanted to take a census of how many armed soldiers he had.

We are not given an explanation except what is found in verse one: *"And Satan stood up against Israel, and provoked David to number Israel."* While it is true that this statement differs from the one in 2 Samuel 24:1

which says: *"And again the anger of the Lord was kindled against Israel, and he moved David against them to say, Go, number Israel and Judah,"* when we consolidate the information from both references we have a better understanding of what happened.

In 2 Samuel the first thing we read is that *"...the anger of the Lord was kindled against Israel, and he moved David against them to say, Go, number Israel and Judah."* God saw something in David's heart that made Him angry (later in 1 Chronicles 21:17 David takes full responsibility for that which provoked God to anger and fully absolves the people of any fault). We do not know for certain what God saw and can only speculate.

One probable view is that God saw pride in David's heart. Dr. J. Vernon McGee however suggests that something else was also involved: *"God was not pleased when David took a census because David was not delighting in the Lord; he was delighting in his own might. So the thing that motivated him to number the people was the awful sin of unbelief. David was trusting numbers instead of trusting God."*1 Even so we must confess that the cause is not made clear by God. As to the involvement of Satan, one view is that *"... the Lord simply let Satan tempt David to undertake the census, much as He permitted Satan to attack Job (cf. Job 1:12 and comments on 2 Sam. 24:1-3). In His sovereignty God's ultimate authority extends even to the workings of Satan. David's immediate purpose was to assess his military strength (1 Chron. 21:5). This incurred divine displeasure because it suggested that he was relying more on his military's capabilities than on God's power. Probably that is why David admitted that his action was sin (v. 8)."* 2

3 *And Joab answered, The Lord make his people a hundred times so many more as they be: but, my lord the king, are they not all my lord's servants? why then doth my lord require this thing? Why will he be a cause of trespass to Israel?*

4 *Nevertheless the king's word prevailed against Joab. Wherefore Joab departed, and went throughout all Israel, and came to Jerusalem.*

Some Lessons About Worship from God's Examples

Joab, who served as David's faithful General over his armed forces in addition to God, questioned the king's motives when given a commandment to number the army because he believed this commandment to be out of order. However, Joab still obeyed the commandment and went throughout the land numbering the armed men who served King David

5 *And Joab gave the sum of the number of the people unto David. And all they of Israel were a thousand and a hundred thousand men that drew sword: and Judah was four hundred threescore and ten thousand men that drew sword.*

There seems to be a contradiction in the given numbers found in 2 Samuel 24 and 1 Chronicles 21, but the truth is the seeming contradiction was borne as a result of the different methods used in the census. In any case the size of David's army numbered over 1,500,000 armed men — quite a staggering number and evidently much larger than anywhere else in the world at the time.

It may very well be that the size of David's army may have been a source of pride as well as a source of dependence for David as Dr. McGee suggested. Whatever the motive behind David's actions may not be known to us, but God saw sin in his heart and David was convicted. The sin was far more serious to both God and David than most people today consider it to be. In both of their eyes it deserved severe punishment and the actions of the King seem to have even affected those over whom he ruled who trusted in his leadership.

7 *And God was displeased with this thing; therefore he smote Israel.*

8 *And David said unto God, I have sinned greatly, because I have done this thing: but now, I beseech thee, do away the iniquity of thy servant; for I have done very foolishly.*

9 *And the Lord spoke unto Gad, David's seer, saying,*

10 *Go and tell David, saying, Thus saith the Lord, I offer thee three things: choose thee one of them, that I may do it unto thee.*

11 **So Gad came to David, and said unto him, Thus saith the Lord, Choose thee.**

Through the prophet Gad, God gave David a choice in how he would be punished.

12 *Either three years' famine; or three months to be destroyed before thy foes, while that the sword of thine enemies overtaketh thee; or else three days the sword of the Lord, even the pestilence, in the land, and the angel of the Lord destroying throughout all the coasts of Israel. Now therefore advise thyself what word I shall bring again to him that sent me.*

David wisely indicated that he preferred to be disciplined directly by the hand of the Lord rather than for God to use some human instrument(s) to punish him. Going by this scripture, it would not be wrong to conclude it is impossible to isolate the consequences of a leader's actions and keep them from affecting the people whom he leads. When a leader sins greatly it is often true that he causes his people to suffer greatly. That was what happened in this instance. Seventy thousand citizens of Israel died because of their King's sin.

13 **And David said unto Gad, I am in a great strait: let me fall now into the hand of the Lord; for very great are his mercies: but let me not fall into the hand of man.**

14 **So the Lord sent pestilence upon Israel: and there fell of Israel seventy thousand men.**

15 **And God sent an angel unto Jerusalem to destroy it: and as he was destroying, the Lord beheld, and he repented him of the evil, and said to the angel that destroyed, It is enough, stay now thine hand. And the angel of the Lord stood by the threshingfloor of Ornan the Jebusite.**

16 And David lifted up his eyes, and saw the angel of the Lord stand between the earth and the heaven, having a drawn sword in his hand stretched out over Jerusalem. Then David and the elders of Israel, who were clothed in sackcloth, fell upon their faces.

Some Lessons About Worship From God's Examples

17 AND DAVID SAID UNTO GOD, IS IT NOT I THAT COMMANDED THE PEOPLE TO BE NUMBERED? EVEN I IT IS THAT HAVE SINNED AND DONE EVIL INDEED; BUT AS FOR THESE SHEEP, WHAT HAVE THEY DONE? LET THINE HAND, I PRAY THEE, O LORD MY GOD, BE ON ME, AND ON MY FATHER'S HOUSE; BUT NOT ON THY PEOPLE, THAT THEY SHOULD BE PLAGUED.

The pain of God's judgment was heavy upon King David, but God did what He considered necessary.

While David was dealing with the pain of God's punishment he received another visit from the prophet Gad with instructions for David from *"...the angel of the Lord"*

(The appearance of The Angel of The Lord was a Theophany, that is, a pre-incarnate appearance of the Son of God. For other such appearances see: Genesis 16:10; 18:1-2; 21:17; 22:11-12; 48:16; Judges 6:16,22; 13:22-23; Zechariah 31:1).

1 Chronicles 21:18 *Then the angel of the Lord commanded Gad to say to David, that David should go up, and set up an altar unto the Lord in the threshingfloor of Ornan the Jebusite.*

The message Gad delivered this time was that David was to build an altar at a specific place — the threshing floor of Ornan the Jebusite. The threshing floor of Ornan was located on Mt. Moriah, the same mountain upon which Abraham had offered Isaac as a sacrifice as well as the same mountain upon which Golgotha is located, the place where our God offered up His only begotten Son. In addition to these interesting facts known by God, God had another reason to specify this place upon which David was to build and altar and offer a sacrifice.

1 Chronicles 21:19 *And David went up at the saying of Gad, which he spoke in the name of the Lord.*

1 Chronicles 21:20 *And Ornan turned back, and saw the angel; and his four sons with him hid themselves.*

Now Ornan was threshing wheat.

1 Chronicles 21:21 *And as David came to Ornan, Ornan looked and saw David, and went out of the threshingfloor, and bowed himself to David with his face to the ground.*

1 Chronicles 21:22 *Then David said to Ornan, Grant me the place of this threshingfloor, that I may build an altar therein unto the Lord: thou shalt grant it me for the full price: that the plague may be stayed from the people.*

1 Chronicles 21:23 *And Ornan said unto David, Take it to thee, and let my lord the king do that which is good in his eyes: lo, I give thee the oxen also for burnt offerings, and the threshing instruments for wood, and the wheat for the meat offering; I give it all.*

Ornan did as would be expected — he was pleased that his King desired to use his property for a place of worship, as a place to build an altar unto the Lord God, and considered it an honor to give it to his King. This was likely part of the reason God instructed David to use this specific place ... He knew the offer that Ornan would make and the possibility that David was being tested as to the sincerity of his repentance.

1 Chronicles 21:24 *AND KING DAVID SAID TO ORNAN, NAY; BUT I WILL VERILY BUY IT FOR THE FULL PRICE: FOR I WILL NOT TAKE THAT WHICH IS THINE FOR THE LORD, NOR OFFER BURNT OFFERINGS WITHOUT COST.*

If God was testing David, he passed the test. He rejected the generous offer of Ornan. He fully understood that he could not offer something as a sacrifice in worship that belonged to another man or even something that did not cost him. David couldn't have been able to offer it to God if it were not his.

1 Chronicles 21:25 *SO DAVID GAVE TO ORNAN FOR THE PLACE SIX HUNDRED SHEKELS OF GOLD BY WEIGHT.*

1 Chronicles 21:26 *AND DAVID BUILT THERE AN ALTAR UNTO THE LORD, AND OFFERED BURNT OFFERINGSAND PEACE OFFERINGS,AND CALLED UPON THE LORD; AND HE ANSWERED HIM FROM HEAVEN BY FIRE UPON THE ALTAR OF BURNT OFFERING.*

Some Lessons About Worship From God's Examples

God liked what David did! God's approval of David's repentant heart and his proper and pleasing offering of his sacrifice was made evident when God furnished the fire, straight from heaven. David purchased the property, not only where the altar was located, but also the entire area around it by paying a sizable sum of money. It was now his and he could and did offer to God that which did indeed cost him something. God was obviously pleased that David refused to take the easy way, attempting to offer something that was not his, and instead paid the price for it before he offered it to God.

1 Chronicles 21:27 *And the Lord commanded the angel; and he put up his sword again into the sheath thereof.*

1 Chronicles 21:28 *At that time when David saw that the Lord had answered him in the threshingfloor of Ornan the Jebusite, then he sacrificed there.*

1 Chronicles 21:29 *For the tabernacle of the Lord, which Moses made in the wilderness, and the altar of the burnt offering, were at that season in the high place at Gibeon.*

1 Chronicles 21:30 *But David could not go before it to inquire of God: for he was afraid because of the sword of the angel of the Lord.*

What lessons about worship can we learn from the example before us in this passage?

1. When we do something out of either pride or faith in ourselves it constitutes a serious sin and an insult to God and He punishes us severely.

2. When convicted by God's Spirit, we must identify what we have done as *"sin,"* accept full responsibility for our actions, and take actions to demonstrate our repentance before we can worship God. David wrote: *"If I regard iniquity in my heart, the Lord will not hear me"* (Psalm 66:18).

3. Sometimes it is difficult for even our close friends to gain access to us because of our perceived self-importance; it is wise and profitable for us to listen to those around us who try to help us and give us counsel.

4. While repentance is an internal, invisible personal experience, if it is genuine it will become outwardly visible to all around us by the actions we take.

5. Sin has to be atoned for by the sacrifice of life acting as substitute for the life of the sinner.

6. According to the example before us, it is not only improper and unacceptable to offer something to God in worship that does not belong to us, it is actually impossible to do so. The inherent truth in this experience has some significant powerful implications for worship services today:

   a. Is it possible for a person to offer music performed and recorded by some other person as one's own offering of worship?
   b. Is it possible for a speaker or preacher to memorize and preach a sermon which has been prepared by another person as an act of worship?
   c. Is it possible for one to take another person's item and offer it to God in worship?

7. If it didn't cost you anything, it's not fit to be offered to God in worship. A sacrifice is always costly.

8. When we offer worship to God that pleases Him, He indicates His acceptance of our worship.

9. David's experience of worship increased his respect and fear of God's holiness. We experience an increase of fear and reverence for God when we worship Him".

THE PERFECT CONFIDANT:

You have somebody you can confide in at all times; someone who will never be ashamed of you nor humiliate you. The unconditional nature of this relationship allows you to express yourself fully, something you may never have been able to do before.

Confidence in God empowers us, energizes us, and strengthens us. It is this confidence in God that makes it possible to achieve and accomplish anything and everything that God the Father sets out before us. Confidence in God drives out fear, doubt, anxiety, and worry, and allows us to exist in a state of assurance.

There are many benefits that we have when we have confidence in God. Some of the more important ones are:

- We have greater spiritual growth and we begin to become much stronger Christians.
- We have greater personal achievements.
- We have greater peace in our lives, and our sense of joy and happiness is greater.
- We also make greater and more powerful impact in the lives of other people. In fact the true believer who has God living within them no longer looks upon people and sees them as the world sees them. Now the believer sees them as God sees them.

Some quotations that speaks and will motivate us to have more confidence in the Lord.

- Prov. 3:25-26 "Be not afraid of sudden fear, neither of the desolation of the wicked, when it cometh. For *the LORD shall be thy confidence,* and shall keep thy foot from being taken."
- Ps. 118:7-9 *"The LORD taketh my part* with them that help me: therefore shall I see my desire upon them that hate me. It is better to trust in the LORD than to put confidence in man. It is better to trust in the LORD than to put confidence in princes."
- Prov. 14:26 "In the fear of the LORD is *strong* confidence: and His children shall have a place of refuge."
- 2 Sam. 22:33 "God is my strength and power: and He maketh my way *perfect.*"
- Ps. 91:2 "I will say of the LORD, He is my *Refuge* and my *Fortress:* my God; in Him will I trust."
- Ps. 91:14 *"Because* he hath set his love upon Me, therefore will *I deliver him:* I will set him *on high,* because he hath known My Name."
- Eph. 3:11-12 "According to the Eternal Purpose which He purposed in Christ Jesus our LORD: *in Whom* we have *boldness* and *access with confidence by the faith of Him.*"
- Phil. 3:3 "worship God in the Spirit, and rejoice in Christ Jesus, and have *no confidence in the flesh.*"
- Heb. 3:6 "But Christ as a Son over His own house; Whose house are we, *if we hold fast the confidence* and the rejoicing of the hope firm unto the end."
- Heb. 3:14 "For we are made partakers of Christ, *if we hold the beginning of our confidence* steadfast unto the end"
- Heb. 10:35 "Cast not away therefore your confidence, which hath *great* recompense of Reward."
- 1 John 2:28 "And now, little children, *abide in Him; that, when He shall appear, we may have confidence,* and not be ashamed before Him at His coming."

- 1 John 3:21 "Beloved, if our heart condemn us not, *then* have we confidence toward God."
- 1 John 5:14 "And this is the *confidence that we have in Him,* that, if we ask any thing according to His will, He heareth us."

CLOSENESS TO GOD:

Having your own altar leads to a feeling of great closeness with the Lord. When a person has to go to a public altar to pray, meditate or leave an offering, it may become impersonal because the space and the altar are shared by so many people. When you have a personal altar, it brings closeness with the Lord and in this closeness you can hear the voice of God. So, closeness with God helps you to hear His voice. "Then the Lord said unto Moses, now shalt thou see what I will do to Pharaoh: for with strong hand shall he let them go, and with a strong hand shall he drive them out of his land.

And God spake unto Moses and said unto him, I am the Lord: And I appeared unto Abraham, unto Isaac, and unto Jacob, by the name of God Almighty, but by my name JEHOVAH was I not known to them. And I have also established my covenant with them, to give them the land of Canaan, the land of their pilgrimage, wherein they were strangers. And I have also heard the groaning of the children of Israel, whom the Egyptians keep in bondage; and I have remembered my covenant. Wherefore say unto children of Israel I am the Lord, and I will bring you out from under the burdens of the Egyptians, and I will rid you out of their bondage, and I will redeem you with a stretched out arm, and with great judgments: And I will take you to me for a people, and I will be to you a God: and ye shall know that I am the Lord your God, which bringeth you out from under the burdens of the Egyptians," {Exodus 6:1-7}.

The process of loving God determines how close you are with Him and how you direct your heart toward Him. The heart that believes and loves the person of the Holy Spirit and Jesus Christ as your refuge, your Saviour, and your strength; a heart that believes that Jesus Christ has given access to the throne of the Father, that you can come close to Him. Your closeness to God has to do with relationship. This type of heart is a heart that has the mind of Christ.

HINDRANCES TO ONES CLOSENESS TO GOD

The general truth is that one's sins separate between him and his God. It seems to be an overly simplistic statement, but this statement is the crux of the broken relationship between God and man. From Adam to the end of time, habitual sin will sever the relationship men have with God (Isa. 59:1-2).

Often people express that they want a relationship with God, but they want it based on their own terms.

When one hears the old mantra, "I know the Bible says, but..." they project terms by which they believe God must abide to establish or engage in any relationship. In reality, many simply do not believe that their lives of sin matter when it comes to having a relationship with God. Sin is a transgression of God's law (1 John 3:4). Whether one commits sins of commission or omission, the result is death to the soul (Rom. 6:23). Repentance and remission of sins past is the only answer to starting a right relationship with God (Acts 2:38). Sadly, preaching on repentance is almost nonexistent in too many congregations these days. It is not uncommon to hear of congregants willfully living in various sins despite being baptized. No matter the sin, if it is not repented of, one will perish (Luke 13:3, 5; Acts 17:30-31).

Too many people are like their ancient counterparts in Israel where the people of Isaiah's day no longer regarded the law of God as important in their relationship with Him.

As a result, they were judged for their sin. The nation suffered constant invasions and threats of slavery. They wondered through the attacks, "Why won't Jehovah save us?" Isaiah explains: "Behold, the LORD's hand is not shortened, that it cannot save; neither his ear heavy, that it cannot hear: but your iniquities have separated between you and your God, and your sins have hid his face from you, that he will not hear" (Isa. 59:1-2).

Dear Christian, remember that God will not hear the prayers of those who regard iniquity in their hearts (Psa.66:18). One cannot continue in sin and expect the grace of God to abound (Rom. 6:1-2). People cannot claim to be in the light and yet walk in darkness (1 John 1:6).

God demands holiness and He will not accept anyone on their own terms, they have to meet His (1 Pet. 1:16). Do not think that you can continue in sin and be in a right relationship with God.

Specifically, there are other things which will cause one not to be close with God. Bitterness separates people from God. The word bitterness can easily be defined as the spiteful sourness that comes from the heart which feels it has been wronged. It comes from an old English word which means "sharp, cutting, angry, cruel, embittered" (Online Etymology Dictionary). God has warned mankind of the dangers of bitterness (cf. Acts 8:23; Eph. 4:31). One of the strongest warnings comes from Hebrews 12 when the writer admonishes: "Follow peace with all men, and holiness, without which no man shall see the Lord: looking diligently lest any man fail of the grace of God; lest any root of bitterness springing up trouble you, and thereby many be defiled ..." (Heb. 12:14-15). The people of Israel were tried at Sinai and they failed the test.

Will those in the church today fail the tests of life?

Bitterness turns to anger and anger to turns to wrath.

Anger makes up a larger part of the word danger. There is danger in anger. The child of God is to "count it all joy when ye fall into divers temptations; knowing this, that the trying of your faith worketh patience" (Jam. 1:2-3).

James concluded with the warning: "let every man be swift to hear, slow to speak, slow to wrath: for the wrath of man worketh not the righteousness of God" (Jam. 1:19-20). Too many, when they are tried, become bitter and angry, and unproductive to God. Beware of bitterness and anger because it separates you from your God!

Certainly the inordinate pursuit of entertainment, immoral relationships, an overemphasis on personal financial gain, and a host of other things can draw a person away from God (cf. Jam. 4:1-4; 1 Cor. 6:9-10; 1 Tim. 6:6-10). May the Christian never grow so attached to this world that his vision is blinded to the more important reality of his heavenly home (cf. 1 John 2:15-17; James 4:4). Remember, there is nothing internal or external that can separate us from the love of God, except ourselves (cf. Rom. 8:34-39). If you, dear reader, do not feel as close to God as you once did, who moved away?"

CHILDREN DEVELOPING GENUINE LOVE FOR GOD:

Regular family altar worship will help your children develop a genuine love for God and a solid doctrinal foundation. Make it a habit to pray and share the word of God together with your children daily before they set out for school. When they are grown, they will have their own fellowship because it would have become a custom to them. They will be joyful in serving the Lord in various capacities to the glory of God.

A boy called Timothy was brought up in the Lord by her mother Eunice who married a gentile. The family altar worship became an opportunity for Eunice his mother to teach her son Timothy the word of God.

You can train your children in the way of the Lord. By the time they are grown and on their own, they would have gotten used to communing with God and acknowledging Him in all their ways. This is an important legacy to commit to your children; a strong foundation of faith and love for the Almighty God. When temptations come their way, they will not depart from the foundation you laid neither will they be carried away by difficulties.

I believe it is good to understand that children are spiritual by nature and are born with a deep devotion to God and His goodness. As parents we can promote the inborn spiritual life of our children and unlock their great divine potentials so they develop a genuine love for God and worship Him daily in spirit and truth.

From childhood a baby will experience the essence of God through the way we talk, hold him and meet his physical and emotional needs. When we are gentle and respond with consistency and unconditional love, we build trust and the baby feels loved and learns that the world is a good place. This "goodness" is now how young children experience God.

HELP THAT YOU CAN TRULY OBTAIN FROM GOD.

With the Lord as your friend, you have access to go to Him, especially when you need help. The Lord knows you so well and knows exactly how to assist you.

God created you in His image to have a personal relationship with you. God seeks an intimate heart to heart relationship with you. There are some very good parents that have friendship with their children, while still being parents. God is your Father but He desires friendship with you too. "And the scripture was fulfilled which saith, Abraham believed God, and it was imputed unto him for righteousness: and he was called the Friend of God," {James 2:23}.

A person you can trust as a friend is a sanctuary of safety, one you will go to without hesitation about any problem. God is such a person and desires that you let Him be that kind of friend to you. "He that dwelleth in the secret place of the most High shall abide under the shadow of the Almighty. I will say of the Lord, He is my refuge and my fortress: my God; in him will i trust," {Psalms 91:1-2}. God desires that you enter into the secret place of His presence where there is fullness of joy.

According to chapter 15 of Saint John's Gospel; the Lord Jesus calls us His friends because He communicates with us. Our relationship with God is the most important personal relationship we can ever have.

Finding Life that's Worth Living:

When you cry out, "God help me," do you believe that there is another fulfilling life ahead? A relationship with a dedicated and loving Heavenly Father changes your worldview from a temporary to an eternal perspective "For our light affliction, which is but for a moment, worketh for us a far more exceeding and eternal weight of glory; While we look not at the things which are not seen: but at the things which are not seen: for the things which are seen are temporal; but the things which are not seen are eternal", {2 Corinthians 4:17-18}. The relationship that you develop through knowing God's Son, Jesus Christ, as your Lord and Saviour renews you mentally and physically.

You can't change the world around you until you change your world. We can choose to live in disobedience to God's plans -- living in sin "For all have sinned, and come short of the glory of God," {Romans 3:23}; or we can ask for forgiveness and thank Jesus Christ for sacrificing His life as payment for our sins.

"And you, that were sometime alienated and enemies in your mind by wicked works, yet now hath he reconciled. In the body of his flesh through death, to present you holy and unblameable and unreproveable in his sight," {Colossians 1:21–22}.

By accepting Jesus as Lord of our lives we are *born again* -- members of God's family -- with the guarantee of eternal life in heaven. "For God so loved the world, that he gave his only begotten Son, that whosoever believeth in him should not perish, but have everlasting life" {John 3:16}.

Making the Right Choice

God is willing to help you "For when we were yet without strength, in due time Christ died for the ungodly. For scarcely for a righteous man will one die: yet peradventure for a good man some would even dare to die... And not only so, but we also joy in God through our Lord Jesus Christ, by whom we have now received the atonement", {Romans 5:6-11}. He loves you so much and doesn't want you to go through this trial alone.

All you need do is to believe. Pray a simple, sincere prayer: "Heavenly Father, I believe Your Son Jesus Christ died on the cross for my sin and was raised from the dead. I confess and ask forgiveness for my sins. Thank You for forgiving me and loving me. Help me to live a new life that pleases you, as a new creation in Christ Jesus. Sustain me through this circumstance. It is bigger than me and I can't do it without you. In Jesus' name I pray amen."

If you decided to become a child of God today, welcome to His family. He will never leave you. Hebrews 13:5b: "For God has said, 'I will never fail you. I will never forsake you.'"

7

The Needs for Building Altar
and the Significance of Altar

THE NEEDS FOR BUILDING ALTAR:

The Christian altar was historically used to offer sacrifices to God. It is important because it represents the presence of God, a place where you kneel in prayer and get in contact with God. It doesn't have to be physical. Christians are encouraged to build spiritual altars in order to have a deeper understanding of God's desires.

Satan likes to keep children of God far from their altar through sin.

When we read the book of Daniel 1, we will understand why a family altar is important. In chapter 1 of Daniel, we can see the method used against these four gentle men. First they were taught to speak their language which was "lingo". Second, they had to read their Babylonian literature. Third, their names were changed. What was the enemy trying to do to them? It is good to know that Babylon means 'confusion' and is a type of this present world. In many ways, the Christian's life is one of exile, in a world that is by and large set against the ways of God. We are to know and consider ourselves as exiles and strangers on earth because this is not our real home! "By faith Abraham, when he was called to go out into a place which he should after receive for an inheritance, obeyed; and he went out, not knowing whither he went...But now they desire a better country, that is an heavenly: wherefore

God is not ashamed to be called their God: for hath prepared for them a city," Heb 11:8-16.

Satan does not want you to understand the heavenly language which is your Father, God's language. He wants to cut you off from your mother tongue, the language God uses to communicate with you. Satan's intention is to introduce you into his own language that you forget "you mother tongue in a foreign country". "Children in whom was no blemish, but well favoured, and skilful in all wisdom, and cunning in knowledge, and understanding science, and such as had ability in them to stand in the king's palace, and whom they might teach the learning and the tongue of the Chaldeans," {Daniel 1:4}. The worst thing that can happen to someone is not being able to understand God's language. I believe the only way to help one understand the language of God is when he has the mind of Christ.

To change someone's perception: When Satan succeeds in changing someone's insight their view becomes different from God's view and their understanding is different from God. In essence, the individual lives' contrary to God's specified way of life. The Babylonian system tried to change the four Hebrew boys perception of life which in turn would have affected their worship of God had this succeeded. Thank God for resolute believers like Daniel who refused to conform to the Babylonian plan of action. What is trying to change your perception? You can be the Daniel of this generation. Do not give up nor compromise your faith in God.

The plan which was put in place was aimed at separating and disconnecting them from their Jewish roots. They tried to brain wash and indoctrinate them into the Babylonian way of life. The aim was to make the Israelites so taken up by the things of Babylon that they would have no time to think of their homeland, customs etc and their God. Having an understanding what the enemy had planned against them, motivated them to build an altar where they would gather together and call on the name of God as they worshiped Him. You can now see a familiar pattern here. You should learn from the ant because the enemies plan is no different for Christians today. The world wants us to be like them but we're can't.

Why did Abraham build all those Altars?

If we look at the life of Abraham through the book of Genesis, we will observe he kept on building altars to the Lord.

Why did he do this? One reason was so that Abraham could return to the spot where God had appeared to him and remember the event; the starting point in one's life is very important. Jesus Christ would have told His apostle to stay where they are for the baptism of the Holy Spirit to come upon them, but He told them to go back to Jerusalem and wait for the promise of the Father. He understands the importance of beginning where you are. There is a phrase that says, "Charity begins at home".

DO NOT EAT GOD'S TESTIMONY:

You need to have evidence of what God has done for you. Many people do not acknowledge what God has being doing in their lives nor do they have records to show what God has done to their generation. Where are the record of the dreams, revelations, and the spoken words of God concerning your journey?

Abraham built altars where God had appeared to him, made a promise to him, or blessed him. He did not want to forget all of the good things that God had done for him. Abraham also did not want to forget where God had blessed him. Every altar was built on the spot of contact between him and God and was not something he carried with him. Abraham built altars to show God's move in his life.

Why not go back today to a place where God blessed you in the past?

An altar must be built for our own benefit:

Many people still do not understand the benefit of having altar. It is possible to live for God with a carnal mind and yet be called a child of God. The carnal mind is the enemy of God and is not willing to be subjected to the leadership of God. To be spiritually minded, one must continually stir up the gift of God within him.

If we keep all the rules of the church, but do not maintain our spirituality by visiting our personal altar, we will find it difficult to have a good relationship with God.

According to the Book of Deuteronomy 28, the people would be blessed only if they obeyed the Word of God. They would be unbeatable as a nation. They would be prosperous in farming, ranching, and family-building. All they had to do was to stay on the straight and narrow path.

I think verse two uses a wonderful description, that the blessings would "overtake" them. Many are running around trying to obtain and overtake the blessings. But here we see the God pattern; when we are obedient to the Word, the blessings will then overtake us.

An altar must be built for the benefit of our children:

A Generation That Did Not Know the Lord

"And also all that generation were gathered unto their fathers; and there arose another generation after them, which knew not the LORD, nor yet the works which he had done for Israel," {Judges 2:10}.

Verse 10 says that after the death of Joshua and those who had seen God's mighty acts, "there arose another generation after them, who did not know the Lord or the work which he had done for Israel." And the result of this ignorance is given in verse 11-12, "And the children of Israel did evil in the sight of the LORD, and served Baalim; and they forsook the LORD God of their fathers, which brought them out of the land of Egypt." And verse 14 then describes the divine response to this idolatry. "And the anger of the LORD was hot against Israel, and he delivered them into the hands of their enemies round about, so that they could not any longer stand before their enemies."

When the knowledge of God is kept in a community, especially by those who have personally experienced God's power, faith is nourished and obedience flourishes. Likewise, if parents allow their children to grow up without the knowledge of God, the children not only grow up in ignorance and unbelief, but are headed for destruction. I believe it is the duty of all parents to teach their children about God and his saving work, so that the next generation will know Him and be saved.

It is God's will that parents assume responsibility to teach their children what God has revealed about Himself. It is the parents who have the first and foremost responsibility to see that their children think correctly about God. The most important school in a child's life is the home school where Dad and Mom are teachers.

I remember my childhood days when my father would call us out every night by 8.pm for night prayer before going to bed. We would pray at 5.am in the morning after we'd woken up from sleep before going to stream to fetch get water. When we come back from the stream, we'd then sweep the house, wash plates and dress up for school. As I have previously mentioned, my parents provided exemplary teaching on altar building through their lives. How many nights did I hear my father pray? How many mornings did I awaken to the sound of my mother's prayers?

A generation that does not know God or is not committed to God is a generation that has not developed a relationship with God. If we expect our children to worship, we must exemplify worship. If we expect our children to give offerings and pay tithes, we must do it ourselves. If we want our children to obey the great commission and be witnesses, we must be involved in outreach. If we expect our children to pray, they must see us involved in prayer. Our homes should be an altar unto the Lord.

An altar must be built for the benefit of the lost.

There are people we love who do not have an altar. They have either never built an altar, or they have allowed their altars to fall into disrepair. They have left the house of the Lord and are living in sin. We must build an altar for those who will not build one for themselves. An altar of remembrance: This is where we ask God to save and bring into repentance souls that do not know Jesus Christ and souls that have backslidden.

What are we doing? The word of God says, "He that wins a soul is wise". Rather than win souls we relax and play games in churches instead of praying. We have learned how to entertain in churches instead of Interceding. Where is the travail of the saints? Where is the groaning which cannot be uttered? Where are the preachers with a fire in their bellies and saints with a passion for Christianity?

The Word says, "And I sought for a man among them, that should make up the hedge, and stand in the gap before me for the land, that I should not destroy it; but I found none," Ezekiel 22:30.

We must have an altar of intercession in our lives for the benefit of the lost!

BUILDING ALTAR IS AN INTENTIONAL ACT:

Abraham communicated with the Lord by building altars for worship. Building an altar is an intentional physical as well as being an intentional spiritual act. While worshiping in front of a physical altar is intentional, so likewise is worshipping in the altar of your heart a spiritual act. On Abraham's return from Egypt, he saw the altar he had originally made and he called on the name of the Lord in worship and thanks. Based on this, the altar reminds him of his relationship with God.

We do not need to build altars with stones or altars that will be decorated with candle sticks and incense or sacrificing animals on them, but we do need to build dedicated altars of prayer and worship in our hearts as a symbol of our relationship with God, Jesus and Holy Spirit. It is noticeable that when Abraham and Lot separated, there was no mention of Lot building an altar to the Lord. Lot was living with Abraham when Abraham got the call of God on his life and was living with Abraham throughout his increase. "Abram took Sarai his wife, and Lot his brother's son, and all their substance that they had gathered, and the souls that they had gotten in Haran; and they went forth to go into the land of Canaan; and into the land of Canaan they came," Genesis 12:5. Lot saw God working in his family's life. He partook of the blessings of Abraham's obedience. But Lot did not build an altar. And from the Biblical account, we see how the distance between man and God can slowly grow when we fail to develop a relationship through which we communicate with the Lord. Lot moved toward Sodom and was living nearer and nearer to Sodom until such a time when he finally got to live in the abominable city. Notwithstanding, Lot seemed content to live in the midst of their evil, "And turning the cities of Sodom and Gomorrha into ashes condemned them with an overthrow, making them an ensample unto those that after should live ungodly; And delivered just Lot, angry with the filthy conversation of the wicked. For that righteous man dwelling among them, in seeing and hearing, vexed his righteous soul from day to day with their unlawful deeds," 2 Peter 2:6-8. Lot did not build an altar. In the end, Lot lost his city, his possessions, his family, his wife, "Remember Lot's wife," Luke 17:32" and sin fell upon his daughters who lay with their father.

Our communication between ourselves and God the Father, God the Son and God the Holy Spirit is maintained through prayer, group worship, and fellowship in the body of the believers. It would be good to answer these questions sincerely. Is my heart an altar of God? Do I pray constantly? Do I worship in faith and obedience, in spirit and truth, as our godly fathers did? Have we not heard or read what the Bible says, "Likewise also as it was in the days of Lot; they did eat, they drank, they bought, they sold, they planted, they built; but the same day that Lot went out of Sodom fire and brimstone rained from heaven and destroyed them all. Even thus shall it be in the day when the Son of man is revealed. In that day, he which shall be upon the housetop, and his stuff in the house, let him not come down to take it away: and he that is in the field, let him likewise not return back. Remember Lot's wife," Luke 17:28-32. If you build an altar of prayer and worship in your life, you will be blessed by the presence of the Most High God.

WHY IS AN ALTAR NECESSARY?

To Worship, praise and communicate with God. Ps 99; 9, Gen.13: 4

'If my people, which are called by my name, shall humble themselves, and pray, and seek my face, and turn from their wicked ways; then will I hear from heaven, and will forgive their sin, and will heal their land," {II Chronicles. 7:14}.

   a.   For thanksgiving – Ps 100:4

b. To make vows and consecration unto God.

c. To live a victorious life Rom.8 ; 37

d. To have a blessed and satisfied life. Ps 24. 5, II Corin.9: 11

e. To meet God for divine intervention and breakthrough.

An Altar brings you closer to God and there is a constant flow from God to you.

THE SIGNIFICANCE OF ALTARS:

An altar should reflect the essence of the person's spiritual development, with God being the center of all.

An Altar is a place that is designed or separated for worship unto God; a place of fellowship with God.

It is a place where praises and prayers are rendered unto God.

An altar symbolizes holiness and represents the presence of God; a higher place where untarnished (spotless, blameless) services are offered to God.

An altar is a place of refuge providing comfort from the troubles of life.

An altar can is a place where intercession is made by inspiration from the Holy Spirit, for the well being of others.

After Abraham was called out of the pagan land of Ur to follow God, he built altars all along his journeys. He, along with the great patriarchs who followed, Moses, prophets, and kings built altars to commemorate their experience of encounters with God. I believe we can learn something from the significance of our altars today by looking at the significance of these altars.

In Genesis 12:6-7, God appeared to Abraham and first promised the land of Canaan to him and his offspring, and there he built an altar. This was at Shechem, located between two mountains, Mount Ebal which means *BARREN* and Mount Gerazim meaning *FRUITFUL*.

AN ALTAR IS A PLACE OF GRATITUDE;

Gratitude acknowledges the source of some good thing. With gratitude, we pause long enough to contemplate a need that has been met and then acknowledge the one who met the need. Gratitude is the act of giving thanks. It is in itself an act of humility by which we acknowledge our neediness and someone else's kindness to meet that need.

To show gratitude as a child of God, is not confined to a day or season, it is an attitude that we need to have and live by daily.

The idea of being grateful centers on two principles: First, God created and sustains life on earth by the abundance of resources and knowledge He provided which most people take for granted. Second, the pride of life makes humans take credit for production of all they enjoy, causing them to forget the very Source of their existence and blessings: "Beware that you do not forget the LORD your God by not keeping His commandments, His judgments, and His statutes which I command you today...As the nations which the LORD destroys before you, so you shall perish, because you would not be obedient to the voice of the LORD your God", {Deuteronomy 8:11-20}.

The Book of Luke 17:11-19 tells us a story about part of Jesus' ministry. According to verse 11, on his way to Jerusalem, he went through the region between Samaria and Galilee and met a colony of ten lepers in a village he went to. The condition of these men was that of misery because of the restriction the law placed on them due to their leprosy - vs.12. The bible in Leviticus 13: 46 declares "The person who has the leprous disease shall wear torn clothed and let the hair of his head be disheveled." The phrase of verse 12, "And they stood afar" emphasizes the restrictions the lepers endured under the law. It was unlawful for lepers to come into contact with normal healthy people, according to rabbinic customs. Imagine being ostracized from your society because of a health condition due to no fault of yours.

In addition to experiencing restrictions under the law, the lepers also endured physical agony. Individuals with leprosy were usually identified by their deteriorating skin. Leprosy was a debilitating disease which usually commenced from within before becoming manifest on the outside.

Luke tells us that one of these lepers was very grateful to have received his healing. When he saw that he was healed, he turned back and saw a reason to praise. He saw the difference, the change wrought by Jesus in his life. To him, this was an opportunity to praise God. Many see a need to pray to God but don't see the need to praise Him.

With a loud voice he glorified God. With the same loudness and intensity he cried for mercy, he glorified God. Many times we cry out loud for help but praise in low tones. The same zeal we seek help in time of trouble should be the same zeal which we praise him. And he fell down on his face at his feet, giving him thanks; and he was a Samaritan. The man in question was not a Jew and was therefore not worthy to be healed by Jesus. But by the grace of God, he was healed and came back to worship the one that healed him unconditionally and got more than the others did. The others were able from a distance to receive from the Lord physical healing in their body while the one who returned to show gratitude had a worship experience in addition to the healing he received in his body. From a distance, God may grant a man physical healing in their body but spiritual healing comes only when we bow down at the feet of Jesus Christ to worship him as Savior and Lord. Gratitude is a glad response from a person who acknowledges grace.

Abram expressed his gratitude to God for the promise given him.

Many do not have a thankful heart. An unthankful heart is an ungrateful heart; a heart that is darkened and does not see the need to worship the Lord. When we fail to give God thanks our minds become clouded and our heart grows dark. In our prayers nowadays, we complain more than we actually pray. This attitude darkens our heart and separates us from God.

We need to know that thanksgiving is more than right thinking. The person who thinks right gives thanks for the things that the majority of people take for granted.

The reason why thanksgiving is so vital to our spiritual growth and development is this; a thankful heart sharpens his minds and senses enhancing his worship to God.

Having an attitude of gratitude is an act of faith. It means you are not afraid of life and its challenges and are happy because of your faith in the Lord God. Thanksgiving is the characteristic of a whole life. It is the appropriate response of one whose daily experience is shaped by the recognition that he stands in debt to God, that his very life and experience of living is a gift from God."

Another significant we see as Abraham began to journey on is that he again built an altar between Bethel meaning *HOUSE OF GOD* and Ai means *RUINS* and again worshipped God. Worshipping together a family in the house of God is another means of keeping us from spiritual ruin. We are reminded by Paul in his letter to the Ephesians that we are not to forsake the gathering together as a means of encouraging one another in the faith.

It was to this altar that Abraham returned after his almost disastrous trip to Egypt. Recall the story of his lies and deception at Egypt that almost cost him his wife had not God intervened. He returned to this place of worship as a sign of *RESTORATION TO HIS FORMER COMMITMENT.*

The implication today is that the fire of our altar could go out if we do not listen to the Lord and choose to walk in the path we have carved for ourselves. In the event of the fire on our altar going out, it is our responsibility to reactivate the fire by going back to God in repentance and doing what He says do.

Of all the altars built by Abraham, the one that must have been the most difficult to build was the one at Mount Moriah. He was told to offer his son Isaac, the son promise, unto God as a sacrifice. Abraham obeyed to the point of tying Isaac to the altar and raising his hand to offer him up as a sacrifice before God stayed his hand. It was at this point God opened up his eyes to see a ram caught in the thicket. The same altar where you are 'tested' is the same place from where your breakthrough comes. It was a moment of testing and Abraham passed the test. "And Abraham called the name of that place

Jehovah-jireh; as it is said to this, in the mount of the Lord it shall be seen," Genesis. 22:14. "The Lord provides." So the *ALTAR OF TEST BRINGS US TO ALTAR OF PROVISION.*

When tested or facing trials, let us go back to the altar where we encounter God who will strengthen, renew our faith and enable us to stand for He is a God that provides. James 1:12 tells us, "Blessed is the one who perseveres under trial, because when he has stood the test, he will receive the crown of life that God has promised to those who love him."

Isaac learned from his father the importance of building altars. "And he went up from thence to Beer-sheba. And the Lord appeared unto him the same night, and said, I am the God of Abraham thy father; fear not, for I am with thee, and will bless thee, and multiply thy seed for my servant Abraham's sake. And he builded an altar there, and called upon the name of the Lord, and pitched his tent there; and there Isaac's servants digged a well," Genesis. 26:23-25.

The spiritual heritage of altar building had been successfully handed down through the generation of Abraham. It was now time for God to lead Moses in embracing the idea of building an altar, according to divine specification for God's purposes. This later became the focal point from where the Hebrews would worship God through prayer, praise, sacrifice and commitment. Altars also served as commemorative structures marking great victories and important passages such as the crossing of the Jordan River into the Promised Land. These were built by both Moses and Joshua respectively.

Gideon defied the priests of Baal by tearing down the pagan altar. On the night before he did this, he first built his own altar as recorded in the book of Judges and named it the *"ALTAR OF PEACE"*. "Then Gideon built an altar there unto the Lord, and called it Jehovah-shalom; unto this day it us yet in Ophrah of the Abi-ezrites, Judges 6:24.

While the temple may have been the crowning structures of altars in the Old Testament right from Noah through Abraham to Moses and all the Hebrew spiritual leaders, the prayers and sacrifices associated with worship at the altars were not superficial acts or insignificant rituals. Man had a need to focus on specific places where God was known to meet his people. And this place of spiritual encounter was for them the altar.

BUILDING AN ALTAR SIGNIFIES HAVING A RELATIONSHIP WITH GOD THROUGH JESUS CHRIST:

When you have good relationship with God, He fights your battles.

Once again, let us examine Abraham's altar and see what we can learn from it.

Reading Genesis 12 helps us understand human history and our relationship with God. Genesis 12 is the first chapter where God called Abram and later changed his name to Abraham with a significant promise which would have significant results on his destiny, "And I will make of thee a great nation, and I will bless thee, and make thy name great; and thou shalt be a blessing: And I will bless them that bless thee, and curse him that curseth thee; and in thee shall all families of the earth be blessed," {Genesis 12:2-3 KJV}.

God's promise is firm; we can see right before our eyes what is happing to nations who rise up against Israel, "And the Lord appeared to Abram, and said, To your descendants I will give this land: and there he built an altar to the LORD, who had appeared to him," {Genesis 12:7}.

Abraham built altars at the same times to ensure his obedience to the Lord and to sacrifice and worship God who called him. When Abraham came back from Egypt, he first went to the previous place he built an altar and there he called the name of the Lord, "And he went on his journeys from the south even to Beth-el, unto the place where his tent had been at the beginning, between Beth-el and Hai: Unto the place of the altar, which he had made there at the first: there Abram called on the name of the LORD," {Genesis 13:3-4}. This is a way of worship and sacrifice to God. When Abraham and Lot separated and Abram moved to the region of Hebron, he built an altar there to the Lord, "Then Abram removed his tent, and came and dwelt in the plain of Mamre, which is in Hebron, and built there in altar unto the LORD," {Genesis 13:18}.

We should not be carried away by all kinds of strange teachings. It is good for our hearts to be strengthened by grace through our prayers and worship to God. The sacrifice of Christ is one that all may partake of in a sense. The sacrifice of animals is now no longer required.

It has been said that the cross is the New Testament "altar" where God offered up the ultimate sacrifice for the sin of all mankind. This was the ultimate Day of Atonement.

Your Bible is your altar which you need to 'visit' every day of your life by reading it during your quiet time in your relationship with the Lord.

A new covenant Christian's altar is Jesus Christ; for it is through Him that we offer our "spiritual sacrifices" to God.

We should be mindful of the type of altar we get involved with and know what is really done there.

There are four powerful factors that can happen at the altar which we should understand.

ALTAR IS A PLACE WHERE YOU ARE STABILIZED

The people had returned to Israel, and they were in a hostile environment, surrounded by enemies. They faced an awesome task, one that may have appeared very discouraging. But before they commenced on any work, they went before God. They built an altar and reinstituted their method of worship; symbolically they returned to God before they returned to work. All projects undertaken for God must always be preceded with a committal prayer to God.

So the altar was a place of stability in an environment of uncertainty.

"Now after these things, in the reign of Artaxerxes king of Persia, Ezra the son of Seraiah, the son of Azariah, the son of Hilhiah, The son of Shallum, the son of Zadok, the son of Ahitub, The son of Amariah, the son of Azariah, the son of Meraioth, The son of Zerahiah, the son of Uzzi, the son Bukki,

The son of Abishua, the son Phinehas, the son of Eleazar, the son of Aaron the chief priest: This Ezra went up from Babylon; and he was a ready scribe in the law of Moses, which the LORD God of Israel had given: and the king granted him all his request, according to the hand of the LORD his God upon him, {Ezra 7:1-6}.

ALTAR IS A PLACE THAT PREPARES YOU FOR SUBMISSION

It is clear that the Old Testament book of Genesis points to the sacrifice of Christ. It couldn't have been easy for Abraham when building the altar for the sacrifice upon which he was to sacrifice his only son. I believe he had mixed feelings when he looked at his son of promise knowing he would soon lose him through sacrifice.

But Abraham submitted in faith to God in all that he did, even to the point of raising his hand in preparation to offer up his son to God. God intervened, as a result of Abraham's faith and obedience. He passed the test, but more importantly, he provided the picture of what God would do in future. At the altar, you submit to God's command, {Genesis 22:1-14}.

Submitting to God is often the hardest of all tasks, yet it's the most essential if we're to be exalted to fellowship with God and benefit from development of our faculties and powers through this fellowship. The act of selfishness degrades, it's immoral. Adopting a submissive attitude toward God and his will, gives the way for the development of those qualities in us which are worth developing, and which elevate us most when they're developed. The closer we are with God, the more understanding we have of Him and the happier and more useful we become.

Submission to God as a Christian is a pre-requisite to enjoying life. Reluctant submission and obedience to God is no submission or obedience at all. Nothing done for God out of a reluctant heart is acceptable to Him. The acceptable mode of service to God is borne out of a willing and cheerful heart. We must overcome a reluctant heart in serving God because the essence of self sacrifice is in effect the sacrifice of the will. The nature of our relations with God depends upon the extent of our submission to him.

ALTAR IS A PLACE OF COMMITMENT AND A PLACE OF SERVICE:

The law was given that the fire must burn continuously on the altar. Nehemiah structured serving God in such a manner that not only the priests served, but the laity and other tribes too through designated tasks such as bringing wood for the fire on the altar. There were appointed times for days that wood was brought.

Joshua admonished the people to both fear the Lord and serve him with all faithfulness. He was speaking about reverential fear where a person recognizes the power and position of the individual revered and accords him proper respect. Joshua begins his "how to commit to God" speech with a call to "stand in awe" of the Lord.

Faithful service to God is not only a matter of heart. It also is a matter of the will. Serving God is not mandatory. Everyone worships something.

Joshua recognized the fact that God gave us the freedom to choose out of His love for us. Love flourishes only when it is given voluntarily. Serving God faithfully is borne out of will.

God wants our hearts and our all. He wants us to love and serve Him. We are to live our lives in a manner pleasing and acceptable to Him. All that God gives to us, He wants us to be willing to give back to Him. In all He does for us, He expects us to give Him praise. God has done more for us than we can ever do for Him, has been more faithful to us than we have been to Him.

8

Broken Altar

When we speak of a broken altar in the New Testament, it is not like the physical altar which was built with stone in the Old Testament. Rather, we speak about individual, group or family spiritual altar. A broken altar is an altar that has been defiled. There are individuals, families, and nations etc that have broken altars. God has an altar of covenant with individuals, families and nations which brings Gods presence; His protection and blessings upon them, "Sing to the LORD, all the earth; proclaim the good news of His salvation from day to day," {1 Chronicles 16:23}. "According to your name, O God, so is your praise to the ends of the earth: your right hand is full of righteousness," {Psalms 48:10}.

There are many negative things in our society we accept and practice which defiles God's altar in our lives, families and nations even in some of our churches. However, just because society approves of something does not make it right in God's eyes.

Factors that defile and cause our altar to be broken:

- **Apostasy:**

Apostle Paul warned the church in the book of 2 Thessalonians about the Apostasy. "Let no man deceive you by any means: for that day shall not come, except there come a falling away first, and that man of sin be revealed, the son of perdition," {2Thessalonians 2:3}.

Looking at Apostle Paul's writing to the church in 2 Thessalonians 2:3 concerning 'apostasy', this means rebellion, turning away, adultery and falling away from the truth.

Rebellion: All rebellion is a demonstration of self-will and is against God. Whether it's a teenager rebelling against authority or an adult turning away from the church, the real issue is our refusal to do what we know God expects from us. Sometimes, to hide or justify our rebellion, we seek to justify it by pointing to our parent's imperfections, two-faced Christians, personal slights and the church's inflexibility. There's no justification for using these reasons as excuse to rebel against God.

Rebellion may be a small area of our life that we refuse to submit to God. God views rebellion and stubbornness as one. Samuel said to Saul, "For rebellion is as the sin of witchcraft, and stubbornness is as iniquity and idolatry," {1 Samuel 15:23}. The only remedy to rebellion is confession and total obedience to God. When we confess our rebellious attitudes and actions, God will welcome us back with open arms like the prodigal father.

Rebellion opens door for the devil and his agents to come into our lives, families and nation to attack us. The Scripture strictly warns us against rebellion, and its consequences are not to be taken lightly. God's Word tells us that rebellion is in the same category of sin as witchcraft itself.

Turning away: "But king Solomon loved many strange women, together with the daughter of Pharaoh, women of the Moabites, Ammonites, Edomities, Zidonians, and Hittites," {1 Kings 11:1}.

We see this pattern of destruction in the life of Solomon; one who possessed such great wisdom. He had a great beginning, perhaps the most blessed of any man in history. His commitment to God wore out, other interests were taking priority. His success at building the temple and his palaces developed into a building passion as he expended all of his resources in rebuilding the cities of Judah and Israel. He was also consumed by his developing relationship with neighboring countries, trading tribute and accepting women as peace offerings. Solomon was so distracted by the activities of his routine that he began to turn away from God. From that point it all went downhill in his relationship with God. We can learn from Solomon's mistakes.

Solomon succeeded in leading a unified nation in peace. Initially, he demonstrated a sincere desire to be obedient to God. Solomon should have passed to his son a united, prosperous and peaceful kingdom. Instead the son inherited a fragmented kingdom. Solomon's personal failure resulted directly in these significant events.

"Thus saith the LORD; Cursed be the man that trusteth in man, and maketh flesh his arm, and whose heart departeth from the LORD. For he shall be like the heath in the desert, and shall not see when good cometh; but shall inhabit the parched places in the wilderness, in a salt land and not inhabited," {Jeremiah 17:5-6}. The Old Testament centers on Israel breaking their covenant relationship with God through disobedience in following other gods and practicing their immorality.

"Else if ye do in any wise go back and cleave unto the remnant of these nations, even these that remain among you, and shall make marriages with them, and go in unto them, and they to you: Know for a certainty that the LORD your God will no more drive out any of these nations from before you; but they shall be snares and traps unto you, and scourges in your sides, and thorns in your eyes, until ye perish from off this good land which the LORD your God hath given you," {Joshua 23:12-13}.

Adultery: What is happening in our society and churches today as a direct consequence of adultery is very sad.

One of the most common images for apostasy in the Old Testament is adultery. "Apostasy is symbolized as Israel the faithless spouse, turning away from God, her marriage partner, to pursue the advances of other gods {Jeremiah 5:7}. Adultery is used often to graphically illustrate the horror of betrayal and covenant breaking involved in idolatry. As in adultery, idolatry does bear a strong similarity of someone blinded by infatuation. "And they that escape of you shall remember me among the nations whither they shall be carried captives, because I am broken with their whorish heart, which hath departed from me, and with their eyes, which go a whoring after their idols: and they shall loathe themselves for the evils which they have committed in all their abominations," {Ezekiel 6:9}.

Adultery is one of those cruel sins of which the pain and destruction strikes twice. It has severe consequences both now and in eternity {Galatians 5:19-21}.

God declared adultery in the Old Testament, as a sin deserving of death.

When God set apart a nation to be His special people, He gave them a set of basic guidelines for living. They were the basis for every other law He would give them. These written laws were a record of the way God expected His people to behave. The seventh commandment God gave His people was, "You shall not commit adultery" (Exodus 20:14). God knew that the heart of humankind would naturally seek to fulfil every desire it longed for and gave these laws to make His holy standards known.

God viewed adultery as being a sin so terrible that it was punishable by death. "If a man commits adultery with the wife of his neighbour, both the adulterer and the adulteress shall surely be put to death" {Leviticus 20:10; Deuteronomy 22:22}. If we ever think that God takes adultery, or any other sin, lightly, we should remember what penalties and punishments He assigned to them.

When we carefully read the New Testament, we observe that Jesus, the Apostles and the entire New Testament writers taught nothing new. They might have taught in new ways, but the laws essentially remained the same. Everything they taught was from the beginning and found in the Old Testament books. This is the main reason why Jesus and the Apostles always preceded their teachings with "it is written," or "the scripture saith," and then proceeded to quote God's written law from the Old Testament.

Based on this, the weight of adultery in the Old Testament is the same as in the New Testament.

- **Arrogance:** Bible tells us those who are arrogant and have a haughty heart are an abomination to Him: "Everyone who is arrogant in heart is an abomination to the Lord; be assured, he will not go unpunished" (Proverbs 16:5).

Regarding our attitudes towards God and our fellow-man, God gives us two promises. First, that the arrogant will be punished (Proverbs 16:5; Isaiah 13:11), and second, "Blessed are the poor in spirit, for theirs is the kingdom of heaven" (Matthew 5:3). For in truth, "God opposes the proud but gives grace to the humble" (1 Peter 5:5; Proverbs 3:34)

* The pretence of religion: "But woe unto you, scribes and Pharisees, hypocrites! For ye shut up the kingdom of heaven against me: for ye neither go in yourselves, neither suffer ye them that are entering to go in," {Matthew 23:13}.

God warned the Jewish people about their idol worship, their unfaithfulness to the commandments and their lack of trust in Him in the Old Testament. In the New Testament the epistles warn us not to fall away from the truth of the faith. Apostasy is a very real and an ever present danger to the body of Christ today.

As Christians, we must ask ourselves, "Is there apostasy in the Christian church today?" Is my church leading its members into "the falling away"? How many souls will be lost because of Apostate teachings?

The only way we can definitely determine that an apostasy is in the Christian Church is by comparing what is being taught within a particular church or denomination to what the Bible teaches. The Bible or Word of God contains all the major teachings that we have incorporated into the Christian Faith.

DEFILED AND DEFILING

DELIVERED BY C. H. SPURGEON,

"Then said Haggai, if one that is unclean by a dead body touches any of these, shall it be unclean? And the priests answered and said, It shall be unclean. Then answered Haggai, and said, So is this people, and so is this nation before Me, says the LORD; and so is every work of their hands; and that which they offer there is unclean."

Haggai 2:13, 14.

THE Prophet Haggai very wisely drew out from the priests a definite answer to certain questions which he put to them. With authority, he could say to the people, "This is what your own priests say and this is what you yourselves believe." This was taking them by a sacred guile and was a powerful way of forcing home the truth of God to their heart and conscience.

According to the 12th verse, Haggai first put to the priests this question, "If one carries holy meat in the fold of his garment, and with the edge he touches bread, or stew, or wine, or oil, or any food, will it become holy? And the priests answered, and said, No." Here is a man who is holy—I mean, ceremonially holy—and is carrying part of a holy sacrifice in the fold of his garments. Now, if he touches anything, will he make it holy by that touch? The priests said,

"No." Indeed, they could not say otherwise. Therefore if a man is himself holy, he simply cannot make another person holy by mere touch. If one who is holy speaks good and does good all the time, will he be able to make others holy by his good words and deeds? Certainly not! It's not possible to change people through acts of holiness. Here is a man who in a legal sense is clean before God and carrying a holy thing in the fold of his garment, but he cannot make that which he touches clean or holy.

The Spirit of God having presented the truth of God through the Prophet in that way, suggested to him to ask the priests another question. "Then said Haggai, If one that is unclean by a dead body touches any of these, shall it be unclean? And the priests answered and said, It shall be unclean." There is such a terrible contagion about uncleanness that he who is affected by it spreads it wherever he goes. Whatever he puts his foot upon, or anything he touches with his hand, becomes defiled thereby. We cannot impart holiness through communication, but we can make people aware of things that make unholy. It is easy to corrupt a person through evil communication. A lewd song may be heard by just one person and yet never be forgotten by that person. A wrong action may not be seen by many, yet just the one person that saw the incidence may have in the process learned something that will remain with them all through their life. The horribly contagious and infectious power of sin, wherever it is displayed, is terrible.

The picture from the story of Haggai is about an unclean man who touches a dead body and becomes unclean; thereafter whatever he touches also becomes unclean.

He cuts a slice off a loaf of bread and the entire loaf becomes unclean. He takes some stew out of a stew pot and the entire pot of stew becomes unclean. Exactly the same thing happens to the cup of wine he touches, the pot of oil he puts his finger into and every other thing he touches. In summary, everything he touches becomes unclean because he is unclean. It would be terrible to be like this man—to make the chair that I touch unclean, pollute the very house I live in, to be unable to shake hands with friends etc or come into contact with anything because of my unclean state. Without a doubt, this is a dreadful picture and is not just the picture of the erring people in Haggai's day, but is tenable and a true life representation of many in our present time; of multitudes who pass for very good people in our society. It can still be said of people today "So is this people, and so is this nation before Me, says the Lord; and so is every work of their hands; and that which they offer there is unclean."

I. THE TERRIBLE UNCLEANNESS.

If you want to fully understand the text, or to have it put into New Testament language, you must look at Paul's Epistle to his son Titus. In the 15th verse of the first Chapter, you get this same picture—"Unto the pure all things are pure: but to them that are defiled and unbelieving is nothing pure; but even their mind and conscience is defiled." They are so impure that everything becomes impure to them. Every man whose heart is not renewed by grace is in this sad and deplorable condition. Note that common things are polluted by men of unclean nature. The Apostle Paul, writing to the Romans, says, "I know and am persuaded by the Lord Jesus, that there is nothing unclean of itself." Nothing which God made that is unaffected by sin is common or unclean of itself, "for every creature of God is good." From the day when Peter at Joppa saw the great sheet let down to the earth, wherein were all manner of four-footed beasts, creeping things and fowls of the air, he was taught a lesson that he needed to learn—"What God has cleansed, that call not you common." There is nothing that God made which can be described as common. To the pure in heart, everything is pure—but unclean men make everything unclean. Things are rendered impure by impure men when they touch and use them wrongfully.

Some may ask, "How can that be?" Common things are rendered unclean when you idolize them, focusing your whole attention on them. If the most important questions of your life are, "What shall we eat, and what shall we drink, and with what shall we be clothed", if your priority is focused on these things, though not evil, they become idols and unclean to you. Every idol defiles those who bow down to it. Bowing down here is not restricted to physically falling down before an object but includes allowing your entire focus to dwell on things rather than on God. Your ordinary pursuits may in themselves be perfectly innocent and commendable if they are followed in line with the word of God, but if your objective is self, you become defiled by replacing this objective with God in your life.

Common things defile by an excessive use of them. An example is gluttony. When a man decides to make his kitchen his temple and his belly his god, he defiles himself. The epicure and drunk degrade themselves when they make their indulgence become their god through excessive use. One can go to this type of excess with all kinds of things. The most common and apparent case is the man who indulges in strong drink. But all other common things are capable of being polluted in the same way—and are continually being polluted.

Others pollute common things in their covetousness. The miser's gold is cankered by his avarice. A person who has a penchant for acquiring land at the expense of others defiles his possessions through his greed.

One who exacts labor towards those who work for him, always demanding more but paying less defiles his trade. He turns his traffic into treason against God. A defiled man, who goes into a good business, defiles both himself and the business by excess greed with the goods God entrusted to him as a steward for the good of others.

Through ingratitude, we can defile the common mercies of this life we're given to enjoy. Are there not many who eat and drink, yet never bless God for what they've received? Or what of those who abound in riches yet never offer any thanksgiving from their hearts to God? They are, as good old Rowland Hill would say, like the hogs under the oak which eat the acorns that fall on the ground, but never lift up their thoughts to the tree from which the acorns come. These ungrateful people are willing to receive all the good things God gives them and are greedy to get more—but the Lord never receives from them even the most minute thanksgiving!

Their hearts are set on the gifts of God but they care nothing for the gracious Giver. Know this, when you receive any good gift and fail to thank God for it; you and everything you own are defiled. We can now see the many ways common things may be polluted by men of unclean nature.

Worse still, holy things are polluted by men of unclean nature. It is sad thing to see how the most sacred things can be polluted by the touch of unholy hands. You may have heard of Voltaire and know something of the character of man. I think nobody surpassed Voltaire in clever blasphemy, yet he wrote to a lady—a lady of whose character the less is said, the better—"My friends say everywhere that I am not a Christian. I have just given them the lie direct by performing my Easter devotions (mes paques) publicly, thus proving to all my lively desire to terminate my long career in the religion in which I was born." Only fancy a man like Voltaire, after blasphemously saying of Christ that he would "crush the wretch," then going to eat "the sacrament," as some call it!

Sad to say every Easter there are many people who present themselves in like manner, who have no respect for the Lord's Day, but feign respect for the day because their "priests" call the day, "Good Friday". They come to the Communion Table when through the year they have not considered Him whose death they profess to celebrate. It is terrible to realize that the innermost mysteries of the Church of Christ are often polluted by godless, thoughtless men who come to the table of the Lord not hesitating to break through that guard of fire—"he that eats and drinks unworthily, eats and drinks condemnation to himself, not discerning the Lord's body."

Let me say this; it is not only the Lord's Table that an unclean man defiles, he pollutes the Gospel by using it as an excuse for sin. Listen to what this sort say, "the preacher proclaimed the mercy of God, so I am going to live in sin." Brute beasts are you to talk like that. Another says, "the minister told us that salvation is all of grace and that a great sinner glorifies God when he is converted, so why should I not be a great sinner?" O horrible wretch, you are accursed, indeed, when you can turn the very Grace of God into an excuse for your wantonness and sin?" Oh, but," says a third, "You say that salvation is all of the Sovereignty of God, therefore I cannot do anything in the matter." You are so defiled that you use the blessed Gospel as the instrument of your rebellion against God. Such people are alas, all too common—they touch with defiled hands the holiest thing and so pollute it.

What happens if these defiled people pray? There are many prayers which only insult the Most High God. As a sinner, whatever posture you adopt, you are still "a miserable sinner," even if you don't believe you are or show remorse for your sin. What you are doing is provoking the Lord to anger by lying about your sin nature in His Presence. It is awful to repeat a form of prayer when your heart does not mean what you are saying. This is a direct insult to the Lord. How then can men who are defiled offer an acceptable prayer to God? They first must be cleansed from their sin before their prayers can be accepted.

Good works are polluted when they come from evil men. See what it says in the text—"So is this people, and so is this nation before Me, says the Lord; and so is every work of their hands." Here is a charitable man—who had been giving away a great deal of money, yet look at how he has defiled his liberality. He sounded a trumpet before him. He was ostentatious; he desired to be thought of as being very generous thus defiling every penny given to the poor! "Take heed," says our Lord, "that you do not give your alms before men, to be seen of them: otherwise you have no reward from your Father which is in Heaven. Therefore when you give your alms, do not sound a trumpet before you as the hypocrites do in the synagogues and in the streets, that they may have glory of men. Verily I say to you, they have their reward." There is no reward reserved for them at the resurrection of the just, for they have had their reward already!

Here is another man, a very religious man though not renewed and regenerate in his way. Why is he religious? Partly out of fear but probably more from custom! He may have intended to please his friends, or maybe to have right standing with his neighbors. These reasons simply defile religion.

I have also known some men who appear very humble in order to gain their desires. When an unrenewed man puts on humility as a cloak, I classify it as devilish. The seemingly humble man who aims at making some gain through his deceitful appearance —the Uriah Heep of the novelist—is one of the most despicable of all people under the sky. Even if the precious Grace of humility is touched by him, he defiles and causes it to appear loathsome in the eyes of men.

The same man then becomes sternly righteous in order to get revenge on his enemy. "I must do the right thing," he says, and he bellows as though it was painful for him to do the wrong he did. But deep within him, he was simply executing his revenge on someone he hated passionately. He just had to exact his pound of flesh or the extract the uttermost farthing of his debt, and then tries to excuse his malice by saying, "You know we must sometimes make an example of wrong-doers." He argues other people may have been charitably foolishly and had passed over wrongs done to them but he has chosen to be a defender of everything that is upright. Truth is he does it to gratify his desire for vengeance. Is not this often the case with bad men? They defile to the last degree even things that appear good.

Friends, the text declares that sacrifices are polluted when offered by unclean men—"that which they offer there is unclean." The lamb, bulls, fine flour, oil which they pour out as an offering at the foot of God's altar are all defiled.

There is what professes to be a public thanksgiving to God, but it is actually a show to the glory of men. Whenever the unregenerate world brings anything to God as a sacrifice, what a wretched mess they make of it! It becomes another occasion for sinning against the Most High. Supposing a heathen comes on Christmas night when professedly Christians are supposed to be celebrating the birth of Christ, but their cups are full of wine and they can scarcely stand for drunkenness? What impression would he leave with concerning Christ?

An unrenewed man cannot do anything in line with the word of God; he always spoils! The sea has often been strewn with wrecks which have been occasioned by the stupidity of merchants—and the world is full of the tombs of men who have been hurried to their graves by other men. Truly did the poet sing—

Thank God the unrenewed men cannot access Heaven! If they could, Heaven's structure would be drastically altered; it would symbolize the making of another Hell. You may do what you like with a man, but as long as he is unclean, he transfers his defilement wherever he goes. This is a picture of any man who has not been born again! It isn't a pretty picture, is it? Were you expecting me to be cute if this is your present state in life? I am not called to please man but God and I pray God's Spirit convicts you of this truth. In your present condition you cannot please nor serve God. You must be born again. "Except a man is born again, he cannot see the Kingdom of God"—he cannot even see it! —And further, "Except a man is born of water and of the Spirit, he cannot enter into the Kingdom of God." He cannot be a subject of that Kingdom until he has passed from death to life—has been made a new creature in Christ Jesus; and has been cleansed from his sins.

II. I have so far kept to my text, but I'm now am going to speak to you about THE ALLSUFFICIENT REMEDY.

Where can we find a better type and figure of that remedy than in the chapter which I read to you just now from the Book of Numbers?

In Numbers 19 we have a type of the great remedy and a striking account of the uncleanness which it removed. I shall not attempt a full exposition of the rites used for purifying the unclean, but I would have you notice that first of all, in order to effect removal of uncleanness, there was a sacrifice. There was a red heifer, without spot, which had to be slain. There could be no purification except through death and there can be no cleansing of your defilement, except through the Sacrifice of the Son of God. The red heifer and the lambs and the bulls under the Old Covenant died to teach people that the punishment of sin was the forfeiture of life—and these creatures died in the place of the offender that he might live. They were all types pointing to the Lord Jesus Christ, the Eternal Son of God who, in the fullness of time, came and took upon Himself His people's sin and stood in His people's place—that He might die—"the Just for the unjust, to bring us to God."

There is no way you can be made clean except through the blood of Him whom God set forth to be the Propitiation for sin. Do not sigh, disregard or pass over this truth, but rather consider this; why should Jesus have died if you could save yourself from sin without His death? And if you think his death is not all sufficient for you, what makes you think your effort can save you? It is sheer blasphemy to think that anything you feel, do, or give, can add to the great Sacrifice of Christ! I pray you grasp this awesome truth and accept the fact there's nothing you can do to earn salvation; absolutely nothing! The price had already been paid, simply acknowledge it, repent of your sins, and ask Jesus into your heart, you now become one with God. This is the great Truth of God—"The blood of Jesus Christ, His Son, cleanses us from all sin." There is no other form of cleansing neither is there a need for any other! Listen to this text and believe what it says—"He was wounded for our transgressions, He was bruised for our iniquities: the chastisement of our peace was upon Him; and with His stripes we are healed." Is that not enough for you?

Turning again to the Book of Numbers, you will notice that the heifer was burned outside the camp after it was killed. Burning outside the camp signified that God hated sin and could not bear to have it among His people. Sin must be put outside the camp and the heifer which bore the sin must suffer and be burned with fire. Jesus when He took our sin also suffered outside the gate. I want you, reading this, to realize sin is a hateful thing—you cannot be purged from it while in love with it. Shut it out of your heart as much as possible! Shut it out from your thoughts! Just as it put Christ outside the camp, you must put it outside the camp. You can't cleanse a man form his sins while he still lives in sin and there can be no possibility of forgiveness while one indulges and delights in sin. You must stop it—it must be burnt as offal, over the wall among the filth and refuse of the city—and be put away altogether from you. Symbolically, you see the Lord slain on the Cross, as if He, too, had been a felon, "made a curse for us: for it is written, Cursed is every one that hangs on a tree."

Looking again at typology, you will observe there was a water of separation. The ashes of this red heifer were to be put into running water—not stagnant, but lively, running water—and a mixture made with it. The mixture was thereafter to be sprinkled upon the people as a water of separation, or purification. Dear friends, you and I must have the Holy Spirit pouring into us the merit of the Lord Jesus Christ to make us clean. There is no other purification for you, except by the Holy Spirit. There must be the water as well as the blood—they must both come to purge the conscience from dead works that we may be clean, like the priests of old, and go into the Holy Place to present acceptable sacrifices to God through Jesus Christ our Lord. You must have the blood to take away the guilt of sin and you must also have the water to wash you from the pollution of sin, that you may be sanctified and set apart to the living God!

You will notice, too, that there was an application of all this with hyssop. Hence David says, "Purge me with hyssop and I shall be clean." Faith is, as it were, that little bunch of hyssop. Hyssop was a small plant, insignificant in itself and of no use except for use in sprinkling. It was dipped into the blood and then the guilty one was sprinkled— or into the water with the ashes—with which the unclean one was sprinkled and made clean. You must have this faith to be saved. The blood of the Paschal Lamb would not have saved the Israelites in Egypt if it had not been smeared on the lintel and the two side posts. The scarlet line would not have saved Rahab if she had not fastened it in the window, to be the mark that her house, with its inhabitants, was to be spared. "Believe in the Lord Jesus Christ, and you shall be saved." It is all you have to do—and this He enables you to do. Just simply believe that Christ is able to save you and repose yourself on that dear heart which was pierced for you!

Put yourself into those blessed hands that were fastened to the Cross and you are saved. The moment you believe in Jesus, your sins are gone—all of them, for there is no halving of sin! There is solidarity in sin—it is one great mass! So that the moment a sinner believes in Christ, all his sins—past, present and to come—are gone, and gone forever. "To come," you say, "how can that be before they are even committed?" Did not Christ die, not only before we committed any sin, but before we had any existence? And yet even then, in His death, He put away the sin of His people. If you believe, your transgression is forgiven—you are "accepted in the Beloved!" And, as surely as you live, you shall one day stand before the burning Throne of God, "without spot, or wrinkle, or any such thing," and you shall have no fear—

"Bold shall I stand in that great day,
For who anything to my charge shall lay?
While through Your blood absolved I am
From sin's tremendous curse and shame."

Beloved, see how simple this deliverance is from impurity. If the impurity was terrible, yet the remedy is so perfect, so complete and ever available, that my heart dances while I talk of it to you.

Finally, this remedy must be applied to our whole nature. Remember that the 19th verse that we read—"And the clean person shall sprinkle upon the unclean on the third day, and on the seventh day: and on the seventh day he shall purify himself, and wash his clothes, and bathe himself in water, and shall be clean at evening." If you, dear Friend, would be clean in God's sight, you must be washed from head to foot—not merely with the washing of water, but with the washing of the Holy Spirit. "What is holiness?" said a clergyman to a poor Irish boy. "Please, Your Reverence," he said, "it is having a clean inside." And so it is—and you have to be washed that way—washed inside, washed in your very nature!

The fountain of your being has to be cleansed; the source of all the pollution is to be made white! How can this be done by any man for himself? This great purification can only be worked by a wonderful work of Grace, by the power of the Holy Spirit. But the Holy Spirit has pledged to do this for everyone who believes in Jesus. It is a part of the Covenant—"

Then will I sprinkle clean water upon you, and you shall be clean: from all your filthiness, and from all your idols, will I cleanse you. A new heart, also, will I give you, and a new spirit will I put within you."

"Oh!" says one, "that would be delightful, but I am afraid that I would fall away, after all." You shall not; there is another Covenant promise—"I will put my fear in their hearts, that they shall not depart from Me." O glorious promise! That crowns it all! I want you dear Friends, to have a faith that can believe God and say, "I have given myself over to Christ to save me to the end, and He will do it. And I commit to Him my soul, not just for the time being, but for the rest of my years. I give myself up never to have any claim to myself, again—to be His forever and ever." What does He say to that? He answers, "My sheep hear My voice, and I know them, and they follow Me: and I give to them eternal life; and they shall never perish, neither shall any man pluck them out of My hand. My Father, which gave them to Me, is greater than all; and no man is able to pluck them out of My Father's hand." You see the double picture—

Christ has His people in His hand, and then His Father comes and puts His hand over the top of Christ's! And all who believe in Christ are totally secure in the hand of the Son and the Father—who shall pluck them from there? We defy earth, Heaven and Hell to ever try tear away any soul that is in the grip of the Lord Jesus Christ! Who would not accept such a glorious salvation as this?

O you who are defiled; come to Him who alone can cleanse you! And when He has cleansed you once, you will have to wash your feet daily you shall find Him waiting to wash them. As you walk with Him, you will not have need again for a complete cleansing as He gave you the first time. "He that is bathed, needs not but to wash his feet, but is clean every whit." May the Lord give you that cleansing if you've not been cleansed before and if you have, rejoice in it with all your hearts. Amen and Amen.

NUMBERS 19; PSALM 51.

Numbers 19:1. And the LORD spoke to Moses and to Aaron, saying.—This ordinance was not given to Moses on Mount Sinai, but in the wilderness of Paran, after the people had broken their Covenant with God and were condemned to die. You know that the 90ᵗʰ Psalm—that dolorous dirge which we read at funerals—is called "a prayer of Moses the man of God." Moses at the time lived among a generation of people who were all doomed to die within a short time in the wilderness. This ordinance was especially appointed to meet the cases of those who were rendered unclean by the frequent deaths which occurred. There was to be a simple and easy way of purification for them—and this chapter means that as much as we dwell in a sinful world, there needs to be some simple and ready method of cleansing available to us that will enable us draw near to God.

2, 3. This is the ordinance of the Law which the LORD has commanded, saying, Speak to the children of Israel, that they bring you a red heifer without spot, wherein is no blemish, and upon which never came yoke: and you shall give her to Eleazar the priest, that he may bring her forth outside the camp, and one shall slay her before his face. This was not a usual sacrifice, for the beasts offered were, as a rule, males—but this was to be a special sacrifice. It was not to be killed by the priest, as other sacrificial offerings were, but the Lord said, "One shall slay her before his face."

4. And Eleazar the priest shall take of her blood with his finger, and sprinkle of her blood directly before the tabernacle of the congregation seven times. This makes it a sacrifice. Otherwise it scarcely deserves the name.

5, 6. And one shall burn the heifer in his sight; her skin, and her flesh, and her blood, with her dung, shall he burn: and the priest shall take cedar wood, and hyssop, and scarlet, and cast it into the midst of the burning of the heifer. All was to be burned and then the ashes, the essence and product of it, were to be preserved to make the water of purification needed to remove those constant defilements which fell upon the people of the camp. So the merits of our Lord Jesus Christ, which are the very essence of Him, are perpetually preserved for the removal of our daily pollution. There was also the essence of cedar wood, that is, the emblem of fragrant immortality, for cedar was an unrotting wood. "And hyssop and scarlet." There must be the humble hyssop used, yet there must be some degree of royalty about the sacrifice, as the scarlet colour implied—and all this is mixed with the blood and the flesh and the skin of the creature, to make the ashes of purification.

7. Then the priest shall wash his clothes, and he shall bathe his flesh in water, and afterward he shall come into the camp, and the priest shall be unclean until the evening. What a strange sacrifice was this, for even when it was offered it seemed to make unclean all those who had anything to do with it!

8, 9. And he that burns her shall wash his clothes in water, and bathe his flesh in water, and shall be unclean until the evening. And a man that is clean. Now we come to the merit of Christ, for who is clean except Christ?

9. Shall gather up the ashes of the heifer, and lay them up outside the camp in a clean place, and it shall be kept for the congregation of the children of Israel for a water of separation: it is a purification for sin. This ceremony does not represent the putting away of sin—that is typified in the slaying of the victims—but it represents that daily cleansing which the children of God need, the perpetual efficacy of the merit of Christ, for this red heifer was killed only once in the wilderness. According to Jewish tradition there never has never been more than six killed. I cannot tell whether that is true or not, but certainly the ashes of one single beast would last for a long time if they were to be mixed with water and the water sprinkled upon the unclean. So this ordinance is meant to represent the standing merit, the perpetual purifying of Believers by the Sacrifice of Christ enabling them to worship God, mingle with holy men, and even with holy angels, without defiling them. In the fullest sense, it may be said of our Lord's atoning Sacrifice, "It is purification for sin."

10. And he that gathers the ashes of the heifer shall wash his clothes, and be unclean until the evening: and it shall be to the children of Israel, and to the stranger that sojourns among them, for a statute forever. That was the remedy ordained by the Lord for purifying the defiled. Now notice what made this remedy so necessary.

11, 12. He that touches the dead body of any man shall be unclean seven days. He shall purify himself with it on the third day, and on the seventh day he shall be clean; but if he purifies not himself the third day, then the seventh day he shall not be clean. It seems to me this may be a revelation of our justification through the resurrection of Christ, which took place on the third day after his death; our being brought into perfect rest, which represents the seventh day, through the wondrous purifying of our great Sacrifice, the Lamb of God.

13, 14. Whoever touches the dead body of any man that is dead, and purifies not himself, defiles the tabernacle of the LORD; and that soul shall be cut off from Israel: because the water of separation was not sprinkled upon him, he shall be unclean; his uncleanness is yet upon him. This is the Law, when a man dies in a tent: all that come into the tent, and all that is in the tent, shall be unclean seven days. Think, what a solemn and an irksome ordinance this must have been. Why, according to this regulation, Joseph could not have gone to see his father Jacob, and be present at his death without being defiled. You could not have watched over your consumptive child, or have nursed your dying mother without becoming defiled, if you had been subject to this Law of God. And everything that was in the tent, or in the house, became defiled, too.

15-16. And every open vessel, which has no covering bound upon it, is unclean. And whoever touches one that is slain with a sword in the open fields, or a dead body, or a bone of a man, or a grave, shall be unclean seven days. This Law was, indeed, a yoke of bondage which our fathers were not able to bear. It was meant to show us how easily we can be defiled. Anywhere they went these people could have touched a bone or come in contact with a grave, and were defiled. You and I, no matter how careful we are, will find ourselves touching some dead works of sin and becoming defiled. It is a happy to know there is a means of purification always at hand. We can always go to the precious blood of Jesus and will once again be washed clean—and be made fit to go up to the house of the Lord.

17-22. And for an unclean person they shall take of the ashes of the burned heifer of purification for sin, and running water shall be put thereto in a vessel and a clean person shall take hyssop, and dip it in the water, and sprinkle it upon the tent, and upon all the vessels and upon the persons that were there, and upon him that touched a bone, or one slain, or one dead, or a grave: and the clean person shall sprinkle upon the unclean on the third day, and on the seventh day: and on the seventh day he shall purify himself and wash his clothes and bathe himself in water, and shall be clean at evening. But the man that shall be unclean, and shall not purify himself, that soul shall be cut off from among the congregation because he has defiled the sanctuary of the LORD: the water of separation has not been sprinkled upon him; he is unclean. And it shall be a perpetual statute to them, that he that sprinkles the water of separation shall wash his clothes and he that touches the water of separation shall be unclean until evening. And whatever the unclean person touches shall be unclean; and the soul that touches it shall be unclean until evening. This ordinance was partly for sanitary conditions. The Egyptians were accustomed to keep their dead in their houses, preserved as mummies. No Jew could do that, for he would be defiled.

Other nations were accustomed to bury their dead, as we once did, within the city walls, or round their own places of worship, as if to bring death as near as they could to themselves. No Jew could do this, for he became defiled if he even passed over a grave. So they were driven to what God intended they should have—that is, extramural interments, and to keep the graveyard as far as they could away from the abodes of the living. The spiritual meaning of this regulation is that we must watch with great care against every occasion for sin and, for as much as there will be these occasions where we stumble and fall, becoming defiled, we must constantly go to the Lord with a prayer like that of David in the 51st Psalm, which we will now examine.

Psalm 51:1. Have mercy upon me, O God, according to Your loving kindness according to the multitude of Your tender mercies blot out my transgressions. There may be some people who think themselves so holy that they cannot identify with and pray this Psalm. I can, for one, and I believe that there are many of you who can join with me. Just let us, for the time being, forget all others and let us come, each one for himself or herself, with David's language on our lips or in our hearts as it applies to our individual case.

2-19. Wash me thoroughly from my iniquity, and cleanse me from my sin. For I acknowledge my transgressions and my sin is always before me. Against You, You only, have I sinned and done this evil in Your sight that You might be justified when You speak and be clear when You judge. Behold, I was shaped in iniquity; and in sin did my mother conceive me. Behold, you desire truth in the inward parts: and in the hidden part You shall make me to know wisdom. Purge me with hyssop and I shall be clean: wash me, and I shall be whiter than snow. Make me to hear joy and gladness that the bones which you have broken may rejoice. Hide Your face from my sins, and blot out all my iniquities. Create in me a clean heart, O God; and renew a right spirit within me. Cast me not away from Your Presence; and take not Your Holy Spirit from me. Restore to me the joy of Your salvation; and uphold me with Your gracious Spirit. Then will I teach transgressors Your ways; and sinners shall be converted to You. Deliver me from blood-guiltiness, O God, God of my salvation: and my tongue shall sing aloud of Your righteousness. O Lord, open my lips and my mouth shall show forth Your praise. For You desire not sacrifice; otherwise would I give it: You delight not in burnt offerings. The sacrifices of God are a broken spirit: a broken and a contrite heart, O God, You will not despise. Do good in Your good pleasure to Zion: build the walls of Jerusalem. Then shall You be pleased with the sacrifices of righteousness, with burnt offerings and whole burnt offerings, then shall they offer bullocks upon Your altar.

HOW IS YOUR WORSHIP BEFORE GOD?

Some people's altar has been broken down as a result of their worship toward God.

"Because my people have forgotten me, they have burned incense to worthless idols. And they have caused themselves to stumble in their ways, from the ancient paths, to walk in pathways and not on a highway, to make their land perpetual hissing: Everyone who passes by it will astonished and shake his head. I will scatter them as with an east wind before the enemy; I will show them the back and not the face, in the day of their calamity," {Jeremiah 18:15-17}.

Worship is supposed to be a celebration of being in a covenant fellowship with the living God. It is a time set aside for the members of the covenant, the believers, to demonstrate their faith by genuine praise and thanksgiving to God. And God arranged the worship of Israel in a way that praise and thanksgiving would be most natural for the people. He arranged it for the three great harvest festivals in the land, barley in the spring, wheat in the summer, and summer fruits in the fall. Because the harvests were a gift from God, the people were by duty bound to bring tokens of their thanksgiving to offer to God at the feasts of Passover, Pentecost, and Tabernacles. And since these were harvest celebrations, they were natural times for the farmers to rejoice--the work was over for the season. Only those who grew up on a farm would know how hard the work is, and how much joy there is when the harvest finally comes in.

When the Israelites came up to Jerusalem to worship, they were to bring animals from their flocks, wheat and fruit from their fields, and whatever other gifts of gratitude they wanted to give to God. God did not need the food to survive, "I will take no bullock out of thy house, nor he goats out of thy folds. For every beast of the forest is mine, and the cattle upon a thousand hills. I know all the fowls of the mountains: and the wild beasts of the field are mine. If I were hungry, I would not tell thee: for the world is mine, and the fullness thereof. Will I eat the flesh of bulls, or drink the blood of goats? Offer unto God thanksgiving; and pay thy vows unto the most High," {Psalms 50:9-13}; Israel was to bring the offerings to God not because he needed them, but as an expression of the Israelite's need of God. Refusing to offer the gifts to God implied God was not necessary to the success of the people, when in fact without him they could not survive.

What they brought had to be the first and the best. Nothing else mattered. It had to be the first-born animal, or the first fruit of the crops or the orchards. God gets his share first, because he is the most important. But it had to be the best--the best firstborn or first fruit offering. To bring God an inferior gift would say that one did not think much of God, for the quality of the gift indicates the value the giver places on the one receiving the gift. That is true in any human relationship, and it certainly is true in the spiritual relationship we have with the Lord.

Anyone who offers God worthless gifts despises the name of the Lord and defiles the altar.

The Lord said through the prophet that they were offering defiled food on the high altar. The altar was the place of sacrifice, and the charge against the people of Israel was that what they offered to God did not measure up to the acceptable standard. The "food" that they brought was defiled or polluted. I believe this is the right time for every human being to ask himself a question, is my service to God up to standard?

One of the reasons why we have a broken altar is that many people are more concerned with 'Power, Authority and material things more than with spiritual values. These people set up an altar of materialism as an object of worship besides God. This idolatrous altar replaces God on the throne of one's heart with the desire for and the pursuit of money and possessions. This type of materialism which some people worship is called "the gospel of the flesh." The Scripture sees this as "covetousness", "For this, thou shalt not commit adultery, thou shalt not kill, thou shalt not steal, thou shalt not bear false witness, thou shalt not covet; and if there be any other commandment, it is briefly comprehended in this saying, namely, thou shalt love thy neighbor as thyself," {Romans 13:9}. "Mortify therefore your members which are upon the earth; fornication, uncleanness, inordinate affection, evil concupiscence, and covetousness, which is idolatry," {Colossians 3:5}. To engage in covetousness is to engage in the greedy desire for more things.

An idolatrous person worships or bows to the inferior, "As concerning therefore the eating of those things that are offered in sacrifice unto idols, we know that an idol is nothing in the world, and that there is none other God but one," {1 Corinthians 8:4}; he renders ultimate devotion to an object of limited value. Therefore, materialism bows to the greedy desire for and pursuit of things and exalts them above the knowledge of God.

Millions bow to images; offer incense, burn candles, pray to, worship, and praise. They sing to images, fast in devotion to images, march around images, cry before images, and wail in appeals to images. Yet these images are destructible. They cannot create or recreate themselves. They cannot redeem their worshipers. They cannot hear the prayers offered or accept the sacrifices to them. They have no true glory!. Yet in the wisdom of men, they are worshiped.

We might say, none of us would ever offer incense to a statue or bow before a god of stone or wood. Our gods are more sophisticated than that. We have gods of wealth, stardom, entertainment, music, athletics, work, power, and a thousand other non-image gods. Yet they are gods because they receive the devotion and glory that belongs only to God. If anything in your life takes the place of utter devotion and dependence upon God, then you have exchanged the glory of the incorruptible God for another god.

Example of Manasseh – When I think about this truth of God changing the unchangeable particularly as it relates to peoples' hearts there is one particular example in Scripture that always comes to mind. It is the story of Manasseh.

Manasseh, in terms of wickedness, was to the southern kingdom of Judah what Ahab was to the northern kingdom of Israel.

2 Chronicles 33:1-9 – Do you realize what an incredible condemnation it was on Manasseh to say that he led {seduced} Judah to do more evil than the nations they had destroyed when they came into the land of Canaan?

The reign of Manasseh was evil beyond imagination. This man, was determined to immerse himself in everything that was forbidden by God. Chances are that if you had been in the same room with this man, you could have felt wickedness emanate from him.

In Deut.18, God lists several wicked sins; all occultic and satanic in nature. He declares them detestable in His sight and goes on to say, anyone who practices them is also detestable in His sight. Well, it is almost as if Manasseh read the list and said, "Oh, so God forbids this; then I'll do it. And God forbids this, so I'll do it too." Every one of them:

Manasseh was an incredibly wicked, perverse, evil and hardened man and one who paid no attention to God's warnings and rebuke as we read in 33:10.

So it is no surprise to read of God's judgment on him and it is a judgment that will make you tremble.

2 Kings 21:10-15 - Now the LORD spoke through His servants the prophets, saying, "Because Manasseh king of Judah has done these abominations, having done wickedly more than all the Amorites did who were before him, and has also made Judah sin with his idols; therefore thus says the LORD, the God of Israel, 'Behold, I am bringing such calamity on Jerusalem and Judah, that whoever hears of it, both his ears shall tingle. And I will stretch over Jerusalem the line of Samaria and the plummet of the house of Ahab, and I will wipe Jerusalem as one wipes a dish, wiping it and turning it upside down. And I will abandon the remnant of My inheritance and deliver them into the hand of their enemies, and they shall become as plunder and spoil to all their enemies; because they have done evil in My sight, and have been provoking Me to anger, since the day their fathers came from Egypt, even to this day.'"

{By the way, who will cause this? Who is it that will bring this destruction & calamity on Israel? Who will plummet the house? Who will wipe Jerusalem like one wiping a dish? Who will do it, not just allow it, but will do it? God! I have no problem declaring God sends calamities.}

So God sends His judgment on Manasseh.

Many individuals and group altars have been broken by individuals and leaders of groups. It is very sad to hear of some church leaders who have defiled the altar of the Church with their familiar spirit. A lot of these leaders calling themselves men of God got involved in the practice of seeking the dead.

So many churches leaders today serve with familiar spirit and they use the means of sorcerers, mediums or necromancers, who profess to call up the dead to answer questions. These individuals are said to have a "familiar spirit" of another dead person and are known as a vessel for the inspiring demon. In actual fact the different voices that come out of a person claiming to call the dead is not that of a dead person but that of a demon spirit. A demon spirit can fake the voice or image of a dead person.

That is why God strictly forbade this heathen practice among the Israelites {Leviticus 19:31}. God said the consequences would result in defilement and excommunication from the community {Leviticus 20:6, Deuteronomy 18:10-13}. The one acting as a vessel or medium for a familiar spirit to talk through was to be stoned to death {Leviticus 20:27}. That was the heavy hand of the law in the Old Testament {Old Covenant}.

Saul, the first king of Israel tried it {1 Samuel 28v3-25}. He went to a sorcerer to call up dead prophet Samuel for some urgent advice. Sure enough Samuel appeared, though it was a demon spirit.

To this day, familiar spirits {demons} are under the control of their master, Satan. They influence people to spread lies and deceit in order to thwart the kingdom of God. Opening oneself to the work of demons is an evil thing: "Let no one be found among you who sacrifices his son or daughter in [a] fire, who practices divination or sorcery, interprets omens, engages in witchcraft, or casts spells, or who is a medium or spiritist or who consults the dead. Anyone who does these things is detestable to the LORD" {Deuteronomy 18:10-12a}.

Some avenues through which demons, like "familiar spirits," can gain entrance into a person's life are divination, transcendental meditation, visualization, necromancy, witchcraft, drugs, and alcohol. These are all activities that believers are exhorted, commanded to avoid. Instead, we are required to be filled with the Holy Spirit, with love, with joy, and with the fullness of life that comes from Jesus Christ. We are also to be on guard, "for our struggle is not against flesh and blood, but against the rulers, against the authorities, against the powers of this dark world and against the spiritual forces of evil in the heavenly realms" {Ephesians 6:12}.

We should be very cautious in this generation. We should read our Bible and ask God for a discerning spirit. There is hope in the New Testament Covenant through repentance for anyone involved in the practice of seeking the dead. If true repentance is made and a complete turning away from this practice, they shall not be cut off from God's blessing.

CONSEQUENCES OF BROKEN ALTARS

CONSEQUENCES IN A NATION WHEN THE ALTAR OF GOD IS BROKEN:

Where the altar of God is, His covenant abides with it. God is the creator of every nation and He blesses all nations according to their measure. God calls us to live in covenant with Him. This covenant is a solemn, personal bond whereby He promises to be our God and we are obliged to live as His people. We are blessed in our faithfulness to Him. But if we forsake the covenant and His ways, we suffer.

The covenant itself has a number of important concepts.

First, God is in charge of everything. Second, God has instituted certain authorities within the family, church and state that serve as representatives between Him and the people under their care. Third, God's Word gives us the rules to live by. Fourth, there are consequences to obeying or disobeying His rules. Fifth, the future belongs to those who are faithful over time.

To live in keeping with these covenant concepts is not oppressive. In fact, it is the way of blessing and life. To live in covenant with God brings happiness and prosperity.

When a nation forsakes God, famine becomes one of the results.

Looking at the case of Israel, Prophet Elijah understood the consequence of the nation's spiritual tumble and disloyalty – they had turned to Baal. They had forsaken Jehovah and attacked His honour by allowing His altar to lie in ruins and shambles while they set up other alien altars.

In the days before King Hezekiah, the nation of Israel was given over to "trouble, desolation, jeering and captivity." What was the reason for such misfortune and calamity? God was angry with them. Look at the deplorable spiritual condition that had brought on His hurt and anger.

*"They have also shut up the doors of the vestibule, put out the lamps, and **have not burned incense or offered burnt sacrifices in the holy place to the God of Israel.** Therefore the wrath of the Lord fell upon Judah and Jerusalem and He has given them up to trouble, to desolation, and to jeering, as you see with your eyes, For indeed, because of this, our fathers have fallen by the sword, and our sons and daughters, and our wives are in captivity, Now, it is in my heart to make a covenant with the Lord God of Israel, that His fierce wrath may turn away from us, My sons, **do not be negligent now!**"* {2 Chronicles 29: 7-11}

In the days of Amos, what was the cause of the earthquake that rocked Jerusalem and made such a devastation that *"the city that goes out by a thousand, shall have a hundred left, and that which goes out by a hundred, shall have ten left to the house of Israel"*{Amos 5:3}? Read through the book of Amos and you will find that it was because they had stopped seeking the Lord. Even the priest in the city had been assimilated into dark wisdom and could not tell the difference. To him, the city church he pastored was a great church as it was flowing with wealth and an overwhelming presence of people. God had to commission a simple farmer from a little village to this high-powered and sophisticated city-church with only one simple message. It was: "SEEK Me" {Amos 5: 4, 6, 8}. It means, *"Rebuild your altars, renew the covenants and start to sacrifice to Me again."*

CONSEQUENCES IN INDIVIDUAL'S LIFE WHEN HE BREAKS THE ALTAR:

When Manasseh, the ungodly son of King Hezekiah, forsook God and threw down His altars, he was bound with 'hooks and fetters,' and taken captive to Babylon (2 Chronicles 33:11). What pathetic relevance this has to 21st century Christianity. Today we have so many avenues of ministry, so many great Christian activities and preachers, yet we are still 'hooked and fettered' in one way or another. The reason why the devil can 'hook and fetter' some believers so easily is because they do not pray, they do not tend to their personal altars and they do not know how to sacrifice to the Lord. This leaves them powerless to say, "No!' emphatically when sin knocks at their door.

Some believers behave like Balaam. They vacillate, they compromise, they entertain and they 'spiritualize' their wrongful moves by saying, *"Wait here, give me some time and I will pray about it."* What need is there to pray over the revealed will of God? When God in His word has clearly told us not to commit fornication or adultery and not to marry a non-Christian, do we still 'pray about it'? What happened to Balaam when he tried to be spiritual and prayed over whether or not he should curse God's people after God had clearly revealed to him that he should not? He gave himself over to the powers of deception. He ended up 'hooked and fettered.' When we go the Balaam way, we too will end up like Balaam, who ended up like Manasseh – 'hooked and fettered!"

"Wherefore the Lord brought upon them the captains of the army of the king of Assyria, which took Manasseh with hooks, bound him with bronze fetters, and carried him off to Babylon" {2 Chronicles 33:11}.

The same thing happened to Ahaz, the wicked grandson of king Uzziah. When he neglected God's altars and turned to other gods, he brought shame and desolation not only to himself but also to the nation.

"Therefore the Lord his God delivered him into the hand of the king of Syria. They defeated him, and carried away a great multitude of them as captives, and brought them to Damascus. Then he was delivered into the hand of the king of Israel, who defeated him with a great slaughter" {2 Chronicles 28}.

God's word rings out loud and clear. How could we have missed it? From one prophet to another, from scripture to scripture and from one tragedy to another, God warned us of the tragic consequences of 'broken altars.' Why are we not hearing? Can't you see that the 'hooks and the fetters' and 'the captivity' {drugs, compulsive behaviour, pornography, etc.} in your life, in your family and in the nation are there because we have neglected God? We have forsaken our personal and private times of intimacy with Him. We have 'pulled our shoulders from Him' and have shown Him our backs instead of our faces.

"Our fathers have forsaken him, and have turned away their faces from the habitation of the Lord, and turned their backs 'on God'. They have not burned incense or offered burnt offerings unto the God of Israel" {2 Chronicles 29:6-7}.

"They have turned their backs unto me, and not their face: but in the time of trouble they will say, Arise, and save us!" {Jeremiah 2:27}. "They have turned unto me the back and not the face" {Jeremiah 32:33}.

What a price the nations of the world are paying for turning their faces away from God. They have instead given Him their backs. We reap what we sow for this is what God declares in Jeremiah 18:17, "I will show them the back and not the face, in the day of their calamity."

CONSEQUENCES IN THE WORLD WHEN THEY BREAK THE ALTAR:

This is the terrible consequence when we show God our backs. In the day of hurricanes, tsunamis, earthquakes, sicknesses and diseases, we try to seek His face but alas, we find only His back. Now we know why in tragedies and calamities, God does not hear. He has His back turned on us just like we turned our backs on Him. Have we not witnessed what is happening in the world today? Which country today is without famine? The world economies are shaky; cost of living is extremely high in every nation. A nation with a 70 % rate of poverty and only 30% well-off is not doing well.

"I am broken with their whorish heart, which hath departed from me" {Ezekiel 6:9}.

The awful consequences of 'neglected altars' has caused even the earth and sea to froth and tremble with sudden earthquakes. Wars abound, economic and political disasters seem to be the order of the day, conspiracy and injustice, incurable sicknesses and diseases.

Through the Bible, through history and definitely through our personal experiences, we know the real reason behind these tragedies, these calamities and these prevailing misfortunes. We know the real reason why the 'hooks and the fetters' have come to nations, to individuals and to the world. Darkness seems to have won over in spite of God's promise that "the light shines in the darkness and the darkness can never over master the light" {John 1:1}. Why has darkness won over in our nations? Looking into this, we need realize that 'the nation's altar', 'family altar', and 'individual altar' are broken.

9

Rebuilding a broken Altar

To repair a broken altar we must stand on the right foundation which is Jesus Christ. "For other foundation can no man lay than that is laid, which is Jesus Christ", {I Corinthians 3:11}.

When we talk about broken altar, it is not that the Lord has been broken, neither have the people been broken physically. But rather, the connection between the people and the Lord has been neglected or defiled and the Altar broken.

Throughout the entire Old Testament, we see the necessity of raising an altar. Under the Law, once a year, the High Priest would enter the holy of holies to sacrifice a spotless lamb on the altar. This was done to atone for the sins of the people. The altar was a place of repentance, forgiveness, and restoration. In the New Testament, the altar serves this same purpose, but not with an actual lamb. When Jesus was crucified, He was the sacrificial lamb that God Himself provided. His substitutionary death, once and for all, atoned for the sins of the entire human race. Those who believe and receive this great salvation are promised immediate forgiveness and eternal life.

The altar of the Lord had been destroyed. Many people in this generation think the Lords altar is no longer relevant to them. They felt it would be better to build a new altar that would suit their taste. They don't like what the Lords altar represents and requirements needed to follow Him.

There are accounts in the Bible where altars had to be repaired. One is in 1 Kings 18:30-38. "And Elijah...repaired the altar of the Lord that was broken down..." After the altar was repaired, sacrifice and prayer was offered and something happened. The fire fell. This in effect represents the burning of an individual, nation and family altar. To repair the family altar, we sometimes have to break things down and clear them out like Elijah did.

David was a busy king. One day, after public worship, "David returned to bless his house." He remembered his house.

We too want to keep our own vineyard and have the fire fall on our family altar. We desire that our children will leave home with a keepsake in their heart; a flame burning in their heart which was ignited in their hearts at the family altar. We want to give them precious memories of the family altar.

If nations, families and churches will become diligent and repair the altar, it will help repair us. If we have a burning family altar, our children's lives will be ignited. There's nothing as beautiful as a holy family gathering around the family altar.

STEPS TO TAKE ON HOW TO REBUILD A BROKEN ALTAR:

1. Submit to God; James 4:7; 2 Cor.10:6. Elijah repaired the altar of sacrifice when it was broken down. To do this, every God's soldier must first be God's good worshiper. If you want Heaven on your part, the broken down altar must be repaired in your heart. Give yourself to God and confess your sins. Nothing can give or restore that peace to you till you build or repair that altar in your heart.
2. Recognize that they exist; John 8:32.
3. Ask God for discernment; Isaiah 11:1-3; 2 Kings 6:8-23; 1 Cor.12:10.
4. Know the reason behind their existence; John 10:10; ; Acts 23:12 and 16.
5. Resist and reject the enemy; Jam.4:7; Col. 1:12; Gal. 3:13.
6. Pray prophetically and aggressively; Ezek. 11:1-13; Job 22:28.
7. Destroy the priest of the altar; 2 Kings 1:9-10; Heb. 12:29; Lev. 10:1-2; Jer. 43:11-13; Isaiah 54:16.

8. Spiritually withdraw your name from, emblems, pictures etc from idolatrous altars; Lev 10:1-2.
9. Move boldly and possess your possession; Obad. 1:17
10. Rejoice, thank and praise God; Psalm 22:3; Psalm 68:1-4; 2 Chron. 20:19-23.

10

Summary

What is an altar in today's context? It is a place where specified times are set aside for the purposes of communing with God in worship, intercession and fellowship. It can be anywhere and at any time and as often as is allowed.

Elijah rebuilt the altar because the altar was where he found his strength; the place of intimacy with the Father. It was a place of sacrifice, where he would sacrifice his personal will and ways to the Lord asking for the Father's will and ways. He would rebuild the altar; not just for those who went before him but also for himself and for the ones that would come after him. When rebuilding the altar, Elijah simply stood and prayed a simple prayer to the Father whom he had a relationship with and knew He would be answered.

Altars are places of worship: In other words, God is calling us to set up places of worship and what we call an altar. The fires of the altar should not go out.

Look at the altar in the tabernacle in the days of Moses. God told them to get a certain kind of wood so that the fire does not die out. If there are people willing to set up altars of worship all over the land, it should become a lifestyle with holiness. It should be a daily prayer. It should be a place of discipline where we cry out to God constantly.

One of the effects of raising an altar in holiness is that it brings down the presence of God. Altars give the gods or God you are serving a legal ground to work in the land. In other words, when you set up a prayer altar to the Living God Jehovah, you are saying, "let your will be done on earth as it is in heaven".

Abraham went on building and maintaining prayer altars all the days of his life and he taught his children to do same. Isaac also built altars.

The strategy did not stop with Abraham. This practice went on from generation to generation. They were purging the land and claiming it back to Jehovah God. They contended with the demon gods ruling the land as they called on the presence of God to come upon the land and remain. They were claiming the land back from the kingdom of darkness back to the kingdom of God. It took Abraham Isaac and Jacob many years to purge the land, and cleanse the firmament above it.

These altars create an atmosphere for God to work with His people. When we set up altars, we create clear lines of communication between God and ourselves and we have unbroken fellowship with God. These altars link up with the throne of God where Jesus is seated and creates open heavens. These are places where we meet and connect with God.

Altars are places of mercy: In 1 Chronicles 21: After David had sinned against God by conducting a census, God asked him to choose one of three evils that would befall him and all Israel. When the plague hit the people, he raised an altar and sought God's mercy. God contained the plague.

Prayer altars open heaven: In Genesis 28 we read about Jacob. He came to Bethel and spent a night there. When he was sleeping, he had a dream where the angels were ascending and descending on a ladder. On top of the ladder, he saw God and was told "I am the Lord God of Abraham your Father and the God of Isaac; the land on which you lie, I will give to you and your descendants... and in you and in your seed all the families of the earth shall be blessed. 15 Behold I am with you and will keep you wherever you go, and will bring you back to this land; for I will not leave you until I have done what I have spoken to you."

When Jacob woke up he said, "This is the gate of heaven". When you pray, the gateways of heaven are opened because of your prayers which will remain as a legacy long after you're gone.

God honours it:

There is nothing other than sin which can withhold the presence of God. We saw that after Abraham came from Egypt; he re-established contact with God at Bethel.

Jacob, Abraham's offspring came after over one hundred years and was a man who did not care for God. He slept at Bethel under an open heaven where Abraham, his grandfather, had raised an altar. Abraham had paid the price in his time for this altar.

Altars open heaven. The benefit of the price you pay today in raising a godly altar of prayer will be enjoyed by your off springs up to the third generation. Many parts of the western world, even though they claim to be 'post-Christians', are today enjoying the blessings of God because of what their fore bears did in seeking God and covenanting the land to Him.

Altars are places of provision: God told Abraham in Genesis 22, "Give me your only child Isaac. Give him as a sacrifice on a mountain I will show you". Therefore, they went up the mountain. Abraham got Isaac, bound him and put him on the altar.

Then he raised his knife to kill him but God called out to him and said, "Don't destroy the child. Now I know you love me indeed. You have not withheld your only son". He provided a ram instead. Abraham called the place 'Jehovah-Jireh', the God of provision.

Altars are places where we can offer our best to God. We have seen in this example, Abraham offered his best. God insisted on the best of the land, the first fruits and the choicest animals for sacrifice.

Altars can contain God's judgment: One of the things that can stay God's judgment over an area is setting up altars of unceasing prayer and intercession. David had offended God and God told him to choose three things: Famine, Plague or to run from enemy. David said, "let us fall in the hand of God" and God hit the land with a plague. When he was enquiring of God the prophet Gad told him "go and erect an altar in Araunah's threshing floor." When he did, God stayed the plague.

We must pay a price to raise an altar of prayer. King David counted the children of Israel and God was angry with him. David went before God and said, "I have sinned before you." God had brought a plague. He was told by God to go to the Threshing floor of Araunah {or Ornan in NKJV} and raise an altar to God.

Many of us are at that place where we don't want to create a fellowship and relationship with God. We are unwilling to pay that price of time, space and energy. We say, "Pastor pray for me, intercessors pray for me". It takes a price to institute altar. David insisted on the full price. He insisted on giving everything to set up an altar. God is calling us on a personal basis so that He can have the legal ground to work from.

Altars bring the presence of God: they are places of mercy, provision, they open up heaven, and they are places where we can offer the best. David said, "I insist on paying the full price". God is looking for people like that. That is why He said of David, "He is a man after my own heart."

Let us cry to God to give us grace to start altars in our hearts, families, churches, ministry, and business, wherever we are. Let us pray that God will give us a burden for prayer and intercession. A burden to gather those who are around us in a prayer altar:

Your heart is the first place of communion between yourself and God. Then the altar grows within the context of a family, a fellowship in the workplace or school or other social place. It can become a church altar, a community altar where more than one churches or fellowships meet, and it can grow to a city or national altar where people meet at specific times and season for the purpose of raising prayer and intercession corporately.

Let the church come together every day and cry unto the name of the living God.

Have community altars; maybe one meeting every month. Let different people from different churches come together to pray and call upon the name of the Lord.

As we raise altars to God from individual to corporate level, God works with us in the context of each level. As you begin, God will deal with issues that affect you individually. As you meet in the family context, God begins to reveal and deal with issues at the family level. It goes on to church, community and national level as each group meets often. Soon individuals, families, workplaces, churches, communities and the nation will begin to be impacted as we win spiritual battles and things are manifested in the physical realm as answers to prayer.

God is calling us today. God wants to make a personal altar in your heart.

True prayer and worship starts in your heart. Your heart should be the first altar to call upon the name of the Lord. We find other gods have been unlawful resident in our hearts. There may be so many idols of anger, bitterness, unforgiveness, jealousy, love of worldly things etc. These make us crowded inside. Work must start within your life. As you yield your hearts, you can pass on the fire to others. We will call on God and surrender our hearts to Him. Paul said in Romans 12:1 I beseech you therefore brethren, by the mercies of God that you present your bodies a living sacrifice, holy and acceptable to God, which is your reasonable, service. It is you first to come as a sacrifice at the altar.

Setting up an altar is not easy. You must be ready to pay the price. We need to offer up our bodies as living sacrifice and everything that is displeasing to him. Your heart is the first altar. That is where God can receive a real sacrifice.

The best you can give to God is yourself. In Hosea 10:12 – Sow for yourselves righteousness; reap in mercy; break up your fallow ground, for it is time to seek the Lord, until he comes and rains righteousness on you. When God says, "I am visiting a land," He needs to find cultivated hearts.

God is saying in Jeremiah 15:19 "if you come back to Me, I will receive you; if you remove the unworthiness from the worthy things you will be my mouthpiece. Many people will flock to you." He promises to use us. It is a time to check our lives.

The first altar is your heart so that wherever you go, the pillar of fire will remain on your life and you will be effective in the land. What comes upon the life that is surrendered to God is a pillar of His presence.

The fire on the altar would consume the whole sacrifice and only ashes would remain. God wants to consume all of our old self so that Christ's life will be seen in us and not us. To do this you need to pull down the strongholds that Satan has built in your lives. "For though weapons of our warfare are not carnal, but mighty through God to the pulling down of strong holds. Casting down imaginations, and every high thing that exalteth itself against the knowledge of God, and bringing into captivity every thought to the obedience of Christ," {2 Corinthians 10:4-5}.

It is time for us to cast off the works of darkness and to walk in the armor of light not giving place to the devil. Too many of us have allowed the devil to build strongholds in us; we have allowed him free reign in our lives to harass, oppress and bring us into bondages. God on the other hand, desires we walk in freedom. God desires to be our rock and stronghold, but sadly, many have unwittingly allowed the enemy to build strongholds in them.

You can still turn your life around by giving your life to Christ and doing His will. As long as you're alive, it is not too late to have a fresh start in life. He is able to restore what the devil had stolen from you over the years. Why not give it a go? Give your life to Christ!

Printed in the United States
by Baker & Taylor Publisher Services